Passionate Learners

Would you want to be a student in your own classroom? In *Passionate Learners: How to Engage and Empower Your Students*, author Pernille Ripp challenges both novice and seasoned teachers to create a positive, interactive learning environment where students drive their own academic achievement. You'll discover how to make fundamental changes to your classroom so learning becomes an exciting challenge rather than a frustrating ordeal. Based on the author's personal experience of transforming her approach to teaching, this book outlines how to:

- Build a working relationship with your students based on mutual trust, respect, and appreciation.
- Be attentive to your students' needs and share ownership of the classroom with them.
- Break out of the vicious cycle of punishment and reward to control student behavior.
- Use innovative and creative lesson plans to get your students to become more engaged and intellectually invested learners, while still meeting your state standards.
- Limit homework and limit traditional grading so that your students can make the most of their learning experiences without unnecessary stress.
- And much more!

New to the second edition, you'll find practical tools, such as teacher and student reflection sheets, parent questionnaires, and parent conference tools—available in the book and as eResources on our website (www.routledge.com/9781138916920)—to help you build your own classroom of passionate learners.

Pernille Ripp is a seventh grade teacher in Oregon, Wisconsin and the creator of the Global Read Aloud (www.theglobalreadaloud.com), a literacy initiative that has connected more than 600,000 students since 2010 through the use of technology.

Passionate Learners

How to Engage and Empower Your Students

Second Edition

Pernille Ripp

Routledge
Taylor & Francis Group

NEW YORK AND LONDON

Second edition published 2016
by Routledge
711 Third Avenue, New York, NY 10017

and by Routledge
2 Park Square, Milton Park, Abingdon, Oxon, OX14 4RN

Routledge is an imprint of the Taylor & Francis Group, an informa business

© 2016 Taylor & Francis

First edition published by Powerful Learning Press, 2014

Library of Congress Cataloging-in-Publication Data
Ripp, Pernille.
    Passionate learners : how to engage and empower your students / by Pernille Ripp. — Second edition.
        pages cm
  1. Effective teaching.   2. Motivation in education.   3. Teacher-student relationships.   I. Title.
    LB1025.3.R55 2016
    371.102—dc23
    2015011561

ISBN: 978-1-138-91690-6 (hbk)
ISBN: 978-1-138-91692-0 (pbk)
ISBN: 978-1-315-68932-6 (ebk)

Typeset in Palatino
by Apex CoVantage, LLC

To Brandon, whose words pushed me when I had no direction and whose love will always be home to me.

Contents

eResources

Several of the tools and templates from the book are also available on our website. The material includes the following:

- Student Questionnaire—Beginning of Year
- Parent Questionnaire—Beginning of Year
- 50-Day Class Reflection
- Quarter 1 Self-Reflection and Grades
- Student Questionnaire—End of Year
- Parent Questionnaire—End of Year
- Fall Conference Sheet for Elementary School Teachers
- Fall Conference Sheet for Seventh Grade Teachers
- Spring Conference Sheet for Teachers
- My Conference Sheet for Student Prep
- Student Preparation Sheet for Conferences
- Spring Student Conference Reflection
- Parent Post-Conference Questionnaire
- Common Misbehaviors and How We Work With Them
- Would I Like Being a Student in My Own Classroom? A Teacher Tool for Reflection

To download those items, go to the book product page, http://www.routledge.com/books/details/9781138916920. Then click on the tab that says "eResources," and select the files. They will begin downloading to your computer.

Foreword

Whenever I meet with Pernille Ripp, she gives me a sense that I am sitting with a kindred spirit.

We first met online a few years ago. It's how I meet many teachers these days. Luckily, I was able to spend some face-to-face time with her over the past two years. She is tireless, committed, and calls it like she sees it. When she mentioned that she was writing this book, I was thrilled. As a long-time reader of her blog, I knew that she has so much to share about the lessons she has learned in her classroom.

Passionate Learners is an important read for all people connected to teaching and learning. The narrative Pernille weaves is that of student, teacher, and mother. Specifically, she makes transparent her own process of transformation as a teacher and lets us into the day-to-day life of a professional educator. While I believe all members of the educational ecology can benefit from reading *Passionate Learners*, this book holds a special power for the practicing teacher who looks at the faces of students every day, determined to create an engaging and caring learning environment.

Passionate Learners asks incredibly important questions of teachers. One of the most difficult pieces of the profession today is keeping up with the pace of change and adjusting classroom methods to reflect the tools and resources available now. Early on, the reader is challenged to consider one of the most important questions any teacher can be asked: *would you like being a student in your own classroom?* Pernille's own answer to this question cracked open the space to approach her students and the minutes of the day very differently. Her honesty and willingness to be changed is refreshing.

Passionate Learners also takes up the critical discussion about giving student voice a prominent role in the classroom. The days of students quietly sitting in rows and listening as the teacher talks are over. Pernille lays out exactly why and how a teacher must approach this important topic. She offers her reasoning for this necessary shift and provides practical examples and suggestions for achieving this goal of giving the classroom back to the students.

Giving up our total control of learning continues to be one of the toughest teacher conversations to have. Pernille has blazed a clear trail for us as we seek to honor student voice and choice and bring it into balance with our own classroom responsibilities.

Passionate Learners also considers the role of relationships with students as an integral part of any robust and healthy classroom. She recounts her own struggles to shift from *teacher as lawgiver* to *teacher as relationship builder*. This is not an easy transition and she heartwarmingly tells about her own journey, with its twists and turns, and how she found her way to a more caring and thoughtful environment.

Pernille does not pretend that these transitions are easy. Instead, she inspires us by laying bare the struggles that led her to a better place in her teaching practice *and* how that professional transformation impacted the students in her care.

What is glaringly apparent in *Passionate Learners* is the paramount importance that Pernille places on reflection as a core part of her professional growth. In each chapter, she invites us into her own thought processes and revelations as she considers her learning journey thus far. None of the work she has done over the past seven years would have been possible without this deep and intentional reflection.

This book provides a framework to begin reflecting on our own classroom practices. It is complete with heartfelt stories, helpful suggestions for shifting our own practice, and the wisdom of an in-service teacher who recognizes the importance of sharing, connection, and reflection as she continues to develop into a master educator.

We need more teachers in the world like Pernille, who question, challenge, and sometimes break the rules—pushing all of us to be better versions of ourselves. She is a force to be reckoned with, and this book will give readers a close-up look at the energy and thoughtfulness she brings to all facets of her life.

Diana Laufenberg has taught social studies in seventh through twelfth grades over the past 15 years. She most recently taught at the Science Leadership Academy in Philadelphia, an inquiry-driven, project-based high school focused on modern learning. Diana blogs at Living the Dream (https://laufenberg.wordpress.com/) and is currently an educational consultant with a focus on collaboration, engaged learning environments and experiential education. Her TEDx talk on learning from mistakes has had over one million views.

About the Author

Pernille Ripp is a former fourth, fifth, and now seventh grade teacher in Oregon, Wisconsin, where she gets to inspire students to take control of their learning journey on a daily basis. She is also the creator of the Global Read Aloud (http://www.theglobalreadaloud.com), a literacy initiative that has connected more than 600,000 students since 2010 through the use of technology. Her work has been featured by Edutopia, *Education Week, School Library Journal*, MiddleWeb, and *Learning & Leading* magazine, as well as in many podcasts and interviews.

Pernille is actively involved in furthering professional development worldwide through the creation of EdCampMadWI and through her work as a trainer, writer, and speaker, both in person and virtually. She writes regularly about what she's learning at Blogging Through the Fourth Dimension (http://pernillesripp.com).

She is a Skype Master Teacher, as well as a Microsoft Innovative Educator Expert for 2015. She is the WEMTA Making IT Happen award recipient for 2015, as well as the 2015 ISTE Award for Innovation in Global Collaboration Award recipient.

Acknowledgments

I never dreamed I would be an author, that my name would grace the cover of a book. Those dreams are left to those who know how to write, surely, and not a girl from a small town in Denmark, who never thought she wanted to be a teacher.

Yet, this book proves me wrong once again. It is not the first time I have been proven wrong, nor is it the last, I hope. Many people told me I should write and to those I owe my gratitude.

My mother, whose strength, fierce dedication, and her passion for teaching and growing as a teacher has been the best role model any teacher or daughter could ask for. My sister, whose strength, passion, and support has made me better. My brothers, whose creative visions and courage in life have taught me to be brave. And the rest of my family and friends that never tire of hearing about yet another crazy cool thing that is happening.

To my school teams, the original one of Mark and Jarod, who put up with me and my ideas on a daily basis, who have shown me what it means to be part of a team, and who always have a minute or five to talk. To the sharks, Katie, Kelly, Deb, Bill, Laura; the big sharks, Shannon and Jason; and everyone else who gave me a second home in the middle school: you have taught me more about having fun in education, the true value of a team, and how to best reach all students than I had ever imagined. To the amazing educators I am connected with, your ideas matter.

To my mentors, Kathy and Melanie, you saw something in me I never would have seen in myself.

To all the people who helped me grow as an author and speaker, thank you for giving me a voice so that I could give a bigger voice to my students.

And finally to my children, the four I get to come home to every night, Theadora, Ida, Oskar, and Augustine, who have given me the best title in the world: Mama. And to all those who I have taught; it is for you that I try to change education. It is your voices I am fighting for. Thank you for making me a passionate teacher.

Introduction: Learning to Break the Rules

I wasn't born a rule breaker. In my hometown of Bjerringbro, Denmark (population 7,390), I did not strive to be a rebel without a cause. In fact, I was your average tomboy, a middle of the roader, the "if only he/she tried" child that we now strive not to label in our own classrooms.

I followed the rules set forth because that is what I was told to do. Society has expectations, and even the smallest child tunes into them rather quickly. Of course there were small rebellions—coming home a few minutes late or "forgetting" to do my spelling words—yet my childhood was not an adventurous one, and my adult life seemed to be kind of middle of the road as well. That is, until I became a teacher in an American public elementary school.

My journey into education is nothing awe inspiring. I did not dream of becoming a teacher all of my life but instead felt myself drawn to it as I hit my early 20s. I knew I wanted to reach children, change them, inspire them, and above all listen to them. And yet, once I had the diploma and teaching job in hand, I followed the rules. Good teachers graded, good teachers rewarded, good teachers told students that if their homework was not done then there would be consequences. Good teachers talked and talked, hoping that they could talk their students into listening to them. I was that kind of good teacher.

In my gut, I knew something was wrong—and yet these were the rules. By signing up to teach, I had signed up for the rules, right? I never stopped to question those rules because I did not see anything wrong with them. Why should I? They had been presented to me by well-meaning college faculty, enforced by some practicum teachers, and written about in the fancy education books I devoured for inspiration. If the rules so obviously worked for others, why not for me?

So I taught like I thought I should. I scolded, waved fingers, told kids to sit still and listen, and above all I wielded my grades—not as proof of great learning, but as tools for compliance.

A few years in, my class was a mixed bag of emotions with various big personalities that needed a lot of love and a lot of patience at times. I started every year the same way: detailing how to get an A, how to earn a class party, how to get on the Awesome Board. Basically, how to be the best students they could possibly be. Yet really all I did was tell them the rules and then tell them the punishment there would be for breaking those rules. How is that for inspiring the youth of America?

At the end of that year I was ready to quit, and not in the "Aah, summer" kind of way, but in the "I quit because I hate teaching" kind of way. I would be sad to see the students go, but even more sad about how I had failed them. I did not feel that I had changed a single kid for the better; I had not inspired, I had not made a difference. Instead, I had given them more of the same: punishment, grades, plenty of homework. And I had definitely ruled my room with an iron fist. I was the center of attention because I held all the knowledge, and the students had to listen to me!

We May Have to Break the Rules

That summer, disillusioned with whom I had become and how far I had gotten from my dreams about teaching, I knew something had to change. Since I could not change my students, I had to change the way I taught. I had to break the rules.

Breaking the rules is terrifying within the public school system, no matter how few or how many years you have taught. We are so indoctrinated with how a traditional classroom should look like—from our college years and sometimes years of experience—that when we bring new ideas, or even just trust our instincts, we often think that what we want to try will never really work. Pressure from districts to conform, from the government to tests, and sometimes even from colleagues, to just stay the same doesn't help as we think about changing our practice. Sometimes we give up before we even make the attempt, thinking the barriers and pushback will be insurmountable.

But that summer I was so close to quitting that I found the courage to break some rules. And what I discovered was this: even the smallest changes can make monumental differences. Trusting yourself and your students, and sharing the power of the classroom with them, can lead to great teaching and learning even within the boundaries of our confining standards, testing obsessions, and mandatory curriculums.

We can change education from within. We can change the way our students feel about coming to school, but we have to take the first step. We can do this whether we are experienced teachers or novices just starting out. In this book I want to tell you about what and how I changed—and how my students changed with me. The little and not-so-little things I did all at once (but that could be done one at a time) so that I could give the classroom back to my students.

Whether you are just beginning or well on your way, I hope this book helps you along your journey toward a classroom filled with passionate learners. At the very least, it will let you know that you are not alone—that there really are better ways to teach and that there are others like you who believe the same thing.

I'll begin by sharing some of the missteps I made in my early classroom days as a result of what I had learned in college, and of not trusting myself. Then let me share what I did to change my whole approach to teaching and how my new approach changed everything for the better. All in the hope that my story will inspire you to change what you do, and support you on your journey just like I was supported on mine.

A Note About the Book's Structure

In each chapter of *Passionate Learners*, I follow a framework: what I thought and did then; what I think and do now; what you can do to begin the shift to more student-centered teaching.

Chapter 1: Now Wait Just a Minute, Mr. Wong

Then: Just Listen to the Experts

Now: You Mean Experience Matters?

Next: What You Can Do, Starting Today

I believed college gave me the foundation I needed to become a great teacher. Now I know that college only gives you enough courage to get you into your job. It will never fully be able to prepare you for what you face as a teacher.

Chapter 2: Would You Like Being a Student in Your Own Classroom?

Then: I Am the Sun. You Are Mere Satellites. Welcome to My Universe

Now: Really, Students—It Is All About You

Next: What You Can Do, Starting Today

I believed that I knew exactly what the students needed if only they would listen and let me give them the knowledge. Now I know that a classroom has to be vibrant for students to invest their time and effort into it. We cannot force children to learn; they have to be partners in their learning journey.

Chapter 3: So You Got the Job. Now What?

Then: Maybe I Could Sort of Change the World?

Now: My Students and I Can Change the World!

Next: What You Can Do, Starting Today

I believed that being new meant I had to follow Harry Wong's advice for the first six weeks of school or I would be doomed. Now I know that students mostly know how to "do" school and we must respect their intelligence as we build community with them.

Chapter 4: It's Not How Your Classroom Looks, It's How It Feels

Then: Did You Get Permission to Touch That?

Now: This Is Our Room, Our World

Next: What You Can Do, Starting Today

I believed that the classroom had to revolve around my needs and that students were temporary visitors granted permission to exist in my universe. Now I believe that the room is there to serve their needs and they own it as much as I do.

Chapter 5: The First Day of School: Who's In Charge?

Then: Don't Smile Until December

Now: What I Can't Wait to Do the First Week!

Next: What You Can Do, Starting Today

What Should You Do the First Week of School?

I believed that if I did not assert my authority and control on the very first day of school, the rest of the year would be out of control. Now I know that what we do in the first weeks of school through communication, listening, and genuine interest sets the tone for the rest of the year more deliberately than any set of rules or expectations ever will.

Chapter 6: Where I Give the Classroom Back to My Students

Then: The Teacher Is the Absolute Authority

Now: Well, You Stumped Me! How Will We Find Out?

Next: What You Can Do, Starting Today

I believed that I was the ultimate holder of knowledge and that students needed my permission to gain it. Now I know that being stumped or pressed for answers by my students is a great thing—that I am not the only vessel of information and that questions should guide our learning.

Chapter 7: Letting Go of the Punish, Behave, Reward Cycle

Then: The Teacher as Lawgiver

Now: Let's Talk About It

Next: What You Can Do, Starting Today

I believed that punishment and rewards was the only way to control a classroom. Now I know that control is not what you want—community is—and punishment and rewards will never build it.

Chapter 8: Common or Not—The Standards Are Always There

Then: Watch Me as I Read This Aloud to You

Now: It's All About the Students

Next: What You Can Do, Starting Today

I believed that lecturing and note taking was the best way to deliver content since I was the mouthpiece for all worthwhile information. Now I know that students have to have an active part in the lesson through exploration or unraveling of the knowledge.

Chapter 9: Homework, Routines, and a Whole Lot of Paper

Then: I Think I Worksheeted Them to Death

Now: Explore, Create, Dream, and Fail

Next: What You Can Do, Starting Today

I believed that homework taught time management, responsibility, and accurately showed what students knew. Now I know that homework can be done by parents, that the child who struggles in class will struggle at home, and that I have no right to take more of my students' time. Time management, responsibility, and practice can be taught in school if we control our curriculum.

Chapter 10: How Grading Destroys Curiosity

Then: I Was Queen of the "F"

Now: I Love My Gradeless Classroom

Next: What You Can Do, Starting Today

I believed that grades were an accurate measure of learning. Now I know that they are subjective and misleading at best, detrimental to learning at worst.

Chapter 11: When Change Happens to Good Teachers

This Is My Most Precious Moment

Then: I Did What They Expected Me to Do

Now: I Do What My Students Need Me to Do. And So Can You

So How Do We Change?

Next: What You Can Do, Starting Today

I believed that there was one way to do school to kids. Now I know that school needs to change, and we have to change it from within. Part of that change means including the voices of our students; school can no longer be done to our kids; school needs to be the place where they eagerly learn for themselves.

If you are a teacher reading this book, chances are you're thinking about change. But whether you need to change and what you need to change is entirely up to you.

Here's what I know: If I had not changed the way I taught and affected my students, I still would have been just fine. Just fine, not great—not inspiring, not life-touching as we hope to be. A just fine teacher. But really, at the end of the day, who wants to be just that?

Now Wait Just a Minute, Mr. Wong

"I wish all teachers knew that we don't think like them." —Justin R.

My mother famously tells the story of how I never wanted to become a teacher, in fact, I am fairly certain I yelled it at her in several arguments throughout my teen years. She, of course, knew better and was therefore not terribly surprised when I declared my love for teaching in my early 20s after a long line of jobs that had meant little to me. So at the age of 22, having already dropped out of college once, I returned part-time in the evening to realize my dream of becoming an educator. As an adult student, attending college in all of my seriousness, I was eager to learn everything there was to know about how to be a teacher.

I wanted to be good, great even, and I studied, I planned, and I reflected my little heart out because that was required to be a great teacher. I knew deep down as I did my practicums and student teaching that I was not prepared, but I thought foolishly that I would feel ready as soon as I had my first job. After all, wasn't that what college was supposed to do?

I graduated, found my first teaching job, and waited patiently for the school year and the confidence to arrive. But the confidence never did. With the days ticking down, I realized that I had very little idea of what it meant to *really* be a teacher.

Then: Just Listen to the Experts

"I wish all teachers knew that we're trying as hard as we can."—Dillon R.

So I clamored for advice, expertise, some source of information (if not inspiration) to tell me what I did not know, and through my search I found Harry and

Rosemary Wong—or rather the Wongs found me as their book was thrust into the hands of every first-year teacher in my first district. "This book," they said, "will give you all of the answers." I thought I was saved. The dog-eared pages and the creases in the spine show my devotion to the best-selling bible for new teachers—*The First Days of School; How to Be an Effective Teacher*. In fact, I loved this book so much that I referenced it, highlighted my favorite gems, and yes, gave it to other new teachers as the book that would make sense of it all.

Armed with a confidence built upon the Wongs, I was the teacher who did the first weeks of school just like they said. After all, their philosophy fit perfectly with what I had been taught in college. Rules, routines, expectations. Tell, show, practice. Repeat. I spent a whole day in my classroom meticulously making a poster detailing what to do if you needed to sharpen your pencil, go to the bathroom, or ask a question. I laminated it and put it center stage in my classroom—ready for the first day of school. Ready to discuss, model, repeat. The Wongs had saved my self-esteem and graciously showed me the path to great teacherness.

That first week was a blur of me building community by using ice breakers! Never mind that I was the only one the kids did not know; we were going to get to know each other even better. Bingo, find a friend, and the toilet paper game all flowed through my room as the students waited for real school to begin, and I felt like the ringmaster of a slightly untrained circus.

I was their teacher, their center of attention, the holder of all knowledge, and I could not wait to whip them all into shape. We actually practiced how to walk in the hallway—never mind that the kids did it just fine with minimal instruction and just needed a simple reminder once in awhile. The Wongs told us to practice even after the smallest infractions, so we left the room early and came back late from specials. We would be perfect silent hall-walkers, the role models for the rest of the school.

And we set up our classroom rules! Except we didn't set them up; I had predetermined them but just led the kids to believe that I was magically coming up with them by paraphrasing their ideas. Thanks for the tip, Harry! The kids were definitely invested, prepared, and ready to learn because Harry told me they would be.

Once routines were set, I blindly started following the curriculum that had been taught the year before me. I read the lesson plans, followed suit, and did exactly what was expected. I joked with the students, tried to win them over with my charm while I wagged my finger at their smallest infractions and punished them into behaving. I managed those kids every which way but loose because that is what I was there to do, and Harry told me I was right.

What baffles me to this day is how the students acquiesced. They never questioned the inane things that I made them do or even attempted to ask why I did them. Already by fourth grade they seemed to be content with the system, knowing what was expected of them—how to do school right and to get that A. Or, at the very least, they knew to not question my authority to my face, that nothing productive would come of it. But I wonder now what they really thought. After all, here was a brand-new teacher, teaching them in much the same way as teachers taught kids on TV Land's classic black-and-white television shows. Did any of those fourth graders wonder why school today was more of the same?

Where the Wongs Were Right

- *Eye contact:* This is one of the biggest tools we have as teachers to establish trust, community, and respect. If you want to tell a child that they matter, look at them when they speak with you. Stop and be present whenever you can, rather than multitask.
- *Be ready:* The Wongs compare teaching to a restaurant and in a sense they are right. We should be as ready as we can be when the students enter our classrooms. However, that does not mean everything should be planned out. Leave room for student input and creativity.
- *Be aware of your body language:* Record yourself! We often have no idea what our body language conveys to our students, so take a video of yourself or have a student do it for you and look at your nonverbal cues.
- *Have a task ready as they enter:* My students get to work right away and they know they have to use their time well to get our work done. This is part of our limited-homework classroom.

Now: You Mean Experience Matters?

"I wish all teachers would be good to students and have patience."—Ben S.

I once believed college gave me the foundation I needed to become a great teacher. Now I know that college only gives you enough courage to get you into your job, it will never be able to prepare you for what you face as a teacher. And while the Wongs have their hearts in the right place, when you blindly adapt someone else's program you start to lose your professional identity. Steal from the Wongs or any other teaching book that is handed to you, even this one. Borrow from the people around you, both

> Find inspiration in others, but do not follow them step by step. If your gut tells you some strategy is not for you, then trust your gut. And if your students tell you something is not working, please listen to them as well.

locally and globally. Read blogs to see what teachers are doing around the world. Find inspiration in others, but do not follow them step by step. If your gut tells you some strategy is not for you, then trust your gut. And if your students tell you something is not working, please listen to them as well.

So as I began my first year of teaching I realized quickly how little I was prepared to teach. I realized quickly that what I didn't learn in college was really quite a lot. I didn't learn how to gain my students' trust, interest, or even attention in a genuine way. Instead, I learned systems of control, of management, of planning that would force students to listen. I didn't learn how to teach a child who consistently gets five hours of sleep every night because they are home alone, scared, or a child who "borrows" snacks to feed his or her siblings, or even the child with too much energy who seems to create trouble at every turn. What I had learned (unfortunately) was that these children were in my classroom to pay attention to me, because that is what children are supposed to do.

I didn't learn how to care about my students; this was meant to be a given, taken for granted. I didn't learn how to strip away all the layers and show the true meaning of the lessons being taught. I didn't learn to adapt on the fly, at the start of a tantrum or the twist toward an interesting conversation. I didn't learn to love them all, regardless of their roughness or demeanor.

I didn't learn to always grow, to be humble, and to realize that this journey is not about my teaching but the students' learning. I didn't learn that there are at least five different ways to explain something—or in my classroom, at least 28, because every student explains it in his or her own perfect way. I didn't learn that often the simplest idea, lesson, or decision can make for the most meaningful moments.

> A great teacher is not something you are just taught to be in college, pushed to be through test scores, or coached to become through observations. It is something you become through your experience and your reflection—by paying attention to your everyday teaching life.

I didn't learn how to be great, or even how to be good. I learned how to save paper, be efficient, and to plan, plan, and plan some more. I learned how to find sources and ask for help, but not who the best people were to ask, and how those people change depending on your purpose. I learned how to plan for the fictitious child with special needs, the child who was hyper, the class that was out of control. There are many things I didn't learn in college, but I am not so sure you can bring all those things to your first classroom anyway. Teaching has to be experienced to be learned, not just read about, discussed, and debated.

A great teacher is not something you are just taught to be in college, pushed to be through test scores, or coached to become through observations. It is something you become through your experience and your reflection—by paying attention to your everyday teaching life. I wish I had been taught *that* in college. How to be contemplative and assessment-minded in the most personal sense—how to trust myself to learn from my (inevitable) mistakes. I was not taught these things in college, and chances are you were not either. Perhaps if we speak out about what we wish we would have known, colleges will listen. Perhaps if we ever teach pre-service teachers ourselves, we will prepare them better for the unplannable. We will teach them to ask the students how they want to be taught.

Next: What You Can Do, Starting Today

"I wish all teachers knew that not all students are alike and most will never be."
—Carolyn G.

Whether you are a brand-new teacher clamoring for advice like I did, or a veteran teacher searching for a better way, there are many things you can do to change your teaching. The first step, though, is the hardest: *facing yourself and deciding what you need to change.*

When I started to reflect on what I was doing to my students, and how I was running my classroom, I was ashamed, embarrassed, and truly astounded that my students had not rebelled. I must have done something right because the students had learned, they had progressed—but not as much as I wanted them to and certainly not in the way I had envisioned when I set out to change the world. They had gathered more knowledge because I had taught them but they had not grown as human beings, nor learned to trust their own voice.

Once I knew I needed to change, it was a matter of choosing what to focus on. Looking back, I was able to see that these were things I wanted to address—things I wished I had done or been able to do my first couple of years. So I said to myself and now say to you (if you need to hear it):

◆ **Stop stressing over your room!**
Our time off should be spent recharging, learning, reflecting, and becoming invigorated to teach again. Now is the time to be doing something that will make you feel better, not laboring over the placement of posters, bulletin boards or classroom design themes. The kids will hardly notice your meticulous placement anyway, and neither will the parents, so give yourself a break. Even if it

sometimes feels like a competition to outdo each other in the hallway bulletin boards, it's not. Remember, it's not how your classroom looks, it's how it feels (see Chapter 4 for more on this).

◆ **Ask more questions.**
Whether you are a novice teacher or one who has been teaching for many years, when you start to change the way you teach, it is not the time to be timid or shy. Ask questions at every turn and ask whomever you think will give you the best answer. This includes students (see Chapter 6 for more discussion on including students in your team of experts). Your teammates are probably some of the smartest and kindest people around, so do not feel that you are a burden or that you should already know everything. Ask what works for them; steal, steal, steal their ideas, but make them your own. And do not be afraid to ask the same question more than once. You will never have all the answers, even if you are a veteran.

◆ **Trust yourself.**
Feel that little tingle in your stomach? While it may be nervous butterflies, it could also be your intuition trying to get your attention. Are you daring to think there might be a better way? No need to panic: absolutely go ahead and use some of the same programs as everyone else. But then spend some time listening to your intuition as well. Take one step and then another as you make it your classroom with your teaching style—not a gray copy of someone else's.

◆ **Allow yourself to fail.**
One of the hardest lessons for me was to realize that I was not perfect right out of the box, that I did not possess every answer, and that there were many, many things I had to learn. This continues to be the hardest thing I face. We think that with years of teaching comes expertise, and yet every set of new students welcomes us with a unique set of challenges. While I may have more tools in my toolbox for teaching all students, I still have to realize every day that I do not have every answer. Make yourself a model of *how to try and fail* with grace. Our students love it when we fail because it shows we are human and that we are learners alongside them. Co-workers love our admissions of failure because they show that we do not think we are better than everyone else and that we are also resilient. To be a great teacher you have to be able to try again and again and always make it better—and be transparent as you do.

◆ **Don't beat yourself up.**
Not everything will be perfect, no matter how good your intentions are. Some days will be amazing, others will not. Every veteran

teacher knows this from experience. What matters is that you always take the time to reflect on what happened and never just move on, chalking it up as a bad day or another sign of your imminent failure as a teacher. There will always be more good than bad days, but the bad days loom larger. When they come around (and they always will, trust me) give yourself a break. You will face enough people trying to tear you down; don't join in the fun yourself.

Smile, love, laugh, share, think, reflect, question. Be kind. Be brave. Be you. Everything is going to be just fine. And find your people—those people who will surround you and support you, who will question you and reflect with you and invite you to do the same for them. Find them and cultivate those friendships that start. Those people may talk you off the ledge one day and admire or inspire you the next. We are stronger together as teachers who collaborate, not compete.

2

Would You Like Being a Student in Your Own Classroom?

"I wish all teachers knew that we are not going to be perfect all of the time."
—Rachel J.

During my second year of teaching, the realization slowly dawned that perhaps college had not provided me with enough foundation to help my students learn all they could learn. By year's end, after I left my classroom feeling deflated; I knew I had to either change or give up teaching. My heart told me to stay, but everything else told me I had to change. Change, of course, can go in many directions, and when we start looking seriously for new ways to do things, it's easy to become overwhelmed.

I wondered: perhaps another resource book would help me change? After all, they had not failed me yet. Yet this time, when I was tempted by another thick volume filled with all the answers, I listened to that tiny voice in my head telling me that it was time to carve my own path, separate from what the experts in the books said. I needed to reflect, not read.

I thought about how I was as a student growing up: slightly rebellious, often bored, and yet wanting to please so very badly. I thought about what I'd loved about school—the hands-on projects, exploration, critical thinking, and discussion. I was a fierce competitor in debate.

Then I thought about what I'd hated, and yes, I know that "hate" is a strong word to use. But there were days from primary school through college when I wanted to walk right out the door, never to return, after the teacher had presented the lesson. Indeed, there were days that I did leave, finding an excuse to hurry out before I fell asleep.

As I worked in my classroom to finish putting things away for the summer, I was deep in thought. Looking at the remnants of the school year, I no longer recognized myself as a teacher or a person. It was time for some deep-cutting honesty.

Then: I Am the Sun. You Are Mere Satellites. Welcome to My Universe.

"I wish all teachers knew what it feels like to be a student/kid nowadays."—Kiley J.

I started with a simple question: "Would I like being a student in my own classroom?" It stopped me in my tracks. With the students gone, the classroom cleaned, and the end-of-year exhaustion fading away, I stood in that silent room and faced an ugly reality. No, I would not like being a student here. No, I would not run joyously into my classroom, eagerly looking forward to whatever the teacher had planned, whatever my classmates would share, whatever I would accomplish.

Mine was simply not the type of classroom I would have thrived in as a child. The realization hit me like a sucker punch. What had happened to my dreams of being different? I should have known better, from my own schooling experience. I had been in many classrooms just like this one—rooms where all eyes are on the teacher at all times, where students sit in rows silently awaiting their turn to speak.

It's that all-too-typical classroom where any group work is forced, and homework is turned in "on the dot" or points are deducted. Where you ask permission to sit somewhere else and all pencils are sharpened during designated sharpening time. That was the classroom I had created after two years of teaching, and, honestly, it was exhausting.

In college my professors had loved my meticulously planned lessons for fictitious children. They had raved about my intention to connect with all kids. So I graduated with a big heart and a big head. I was going to save the world. I would be different. I would listen and be in tune with all of my students.

And yet, something didn't transfer from the college me to the teacher me. Once I was inside my classroom with the door closed, I would scold the children when I lost their interest, not realizing that it was my doing. I would raise my voice, tell them to listen up because this might be on the test and that this was important, all in an effort to frighten them into paying attention or at least startle them awake.

Yet the truth was that what I was saying was not important. They could have read it themselves. And the test didn't matter, really, since they could see no connection to their outside life—and grades in primary school do not matter for college, as a child pointed out. Still I droned on, frustrated that their inattention meant I had to repeat directions, frustrated that they were obviously dozing or daydreaming during my lecture, frustrated that their test scores did not show how hard I had worked on preparing them to take it.

What I had failed to reflect on was fundamental. Who was the center of attention in the room? It was not supposed to be me; it should have been the students. But somewhere in my quest to become a really stellar educator, I had confused learning with paying rapt attention to the teacher. I had confused a well-functioning classroom with one where the teacher stood at the helm of the learning ship at all times, surveying and barking orders at the crew.

When we teachers talk a lot (and most teachers love to talk), students turn into drones. Instead of creating opportunities for them to explore the content and discover their own passionate interests, we talk and talk and talk so that we can cover all of the curriculum and get them ready for the Assessment. We talk to get them ready to learn, and then we talk about the learning they are doing, and then we talk about what they've just learned. I had never considered that being quiet might actually help them learn more, better and faster.

I never used to be quiet. My classroom was filled with noise from the moment the students arrived until they left. Whether it was me lecturing, me giving out directions, me keeping them on track, or even a soundtrack of music to keep them motivated, we just didn't do quiet. We were loud, we were active, and there was always chatter.

One night, as I yelled at my husband to turn off his music so that I could concentrate on writing, it finally dawned on me. Perhaps my students didn't need more noise: perhaps they needed more quiet. Perhaps I needed to stop talking, perhaps I needed to stop playing the music. Perhaps I needed to embrace the quiet and let it speak for itself. Perhaps I needed to be quiet so my students could start speaking.

Now, we are quiet when we need to be. During reading, you will hear hushed conversations, during writing it is almost silent. I keep my discussions short. I try to pull my voice out of the conversation so that my students can figure it out among themselves. When a child faces me with a problem I sit quietly and think with them, trying to come up with a solution. When a child is the most unruly and angry, my lower voice and quiet words often diffuse the situation better than any punishment ever could.

Sure there are words, but the quiet now emphasizes them. No longer do I feel the need to constantly yell over the noise. No longer do I feel the need to bark out orders. Sure there are instructions being given, but there is also quiet so they can figure it out. Quiet so they can think. Quiet so they can just be.

All of these early summer thoughts were propelling me toward a breakdown. My pending teacher crisis really gathered steam when I picked up a parent magazine in which this question was posed: "My child dreads going back to school. What should I do?" The answer? "Remind them that they will see their friends and how much fun they will have during recess, art, and music class."

Recess? Art? Music? What about writing, reading, math? What about all the time they spent with me in my room? What about us? Would my next set of students be kids who dreaded our time together, watching the minutes tick by until they could get to the fun part of school? I had to do something.

Now: Really, Students—It Is All About You

"Students should have a chance to decide what they are learning because if they don't like what they are learning about, they will not be engaged in the classroom learning."
—Annabelle B.

I believed that I knew exactly what the students needed if only they would let me give them the knowledge. Now I know that a classroom has to be vibrant for students to invest their time and effort into it. We cannot force children to learn, not even with the harshest punishments. Instead, we have to cultivate their already preexisting love of learning and find ways for them to take ownership over it. This, I believe, is vital to the survival of a child's curiosity.

One child I had taught my first year was obsessed with making movies. This was in 2008, before much of the easy movie making software was available. Yet he had taken the time to figure out how to make elaborate Lego stop-motion movies that he loved sharing with his classmates. He had asked me if he could make a movie for each monthly book report I required.

Instead of enthusiastically giving him permission to further his craft while fulfilling my requirements, I told him no. He needed to expand his skills and create other ways to report on the book, I said.

The teacher me now cringes at the memory of just how downtrodden this kid looked after my answer. He had a passion and a gift for telling stories through movies, and yet I shut it down because it did not meet my narrow book report guidelines. I am sure he would have made quite magnificent movies if the one he was allowed to make was any sign of what he could do.

The first thing I had to do, then, was to share control with my students and not be holding the reins at all times. While this sounds easy, I believe it is a scary proposition to many of us. I imagined my classroom erupting into chaos, and visions of children doing nothing constructive surfaced again and again as I thought about change. In fact, this vision continues to haunt me as I start off another school year, whether it be elementary or middle school, by giving my students control. Yet, every year I am reminded by my students that my trust in them is not misplaced, nor is it too much to expect.

What happened could not have been further from my fears. The students reveled in the notion that they had a say. Cautiously at first, afraid that I did not really mean it, they approached me to ask permission for very simple things. Could they sit on the carpet and work? Could they work with a partner? Could they show me mastery of a concept in a different way?

Yes, they could. And I encouraged them to think deeper and to see what else they could control. Their level of trust grew day by day, even though the old me once in a while reared her ever-so-domineering head. It was a battle to give up some of the control, and yes, there are days where it still is. After all, no one, no matter how experienced, makes the right choice every single time.

Sometimes the students chose the wrong partner, and the old teacher in me wanted to put a stop to it. Sometimes they did not do exactly what I had hoped, and I wanted to give them specific guidelines so that it would be a perfect project. Sometimes they didn't ask the questions I had planned that they would, and I had to hold back from steering the conversation into my territory.

Other times, the learning seemed to explode out of innocent questions, and we would become caught in a frenzy of exploration. Sometimes partnerships that I would never have picked worked better than any others. Sometimes the kids just proved me wrong.

Next step: I needed to stop talking. Brain research tells us that students pay proper attention for about the same number of minutes as their age. If I am teaching 10-year-olds, I get exactly 10 minutes of their time. Now, in a seventh grade classroom, that means 13 precious minutes if the conditions are right. That's it. If I continue to talk, even the sharpest or most compliant students will not be able to sustain their attention.

Immediately upon making the decision to stop talking so much, the doubts came. How would they ever learn what they needed to learn if they didn't listen to me? We didn't have all of the time in the world. We had so much to cover. At this point I really had to trust myself and my intuition that there were different and better ways to learn.

Just like anxious parents who literally force themselves to let go of their child on a bicycle, I had to let go of my own ego. I had to realize that students brought inherent knowledge and curiosity with them into the room and that I was there to facilitate and help them grow

> The best way for the students to learn is to have the time to explore, try, fail, or succeed, and then explore some more.

that knowledge. The best way for students to learn is to have the time to explore, try, fail, or succeed, and then explore some more. They have to have time to talk and think aloud. They have to have time to learn how to pursue questions and run into problems, only to solve them themselves. They have to be given a framework that they can operate within, yet still reach our determined end goal.

School was not all about me, or the knowledge I was going to impart. It was mostly about them, the students. I had already had my turn in school, now it was their turn. And I wanted to make it better than mine.

Next: What You Can Do, Starting Today

"If a teacher is not sympathetic they should at least understand what is going on in the student's life. (Not only that, but it is okay to laugh really hard in the middle of class)."
—Sophie N.

Once again, reflection is where we begin. Ask yourself, would you like being a student in your own room? And if you are not sure, why don't you ask a former student? Perhaps there are elements to your room that you thoroughly enjoy, but look closely and deeply; how is the whole year experienced by your students? How much do you talk? How many rules do you have? What are the routines? Are students excited to come into your room or tired and slow? All of these things are clues to what you perhaps need to change. Starting with the questions is always the hardest part. But be honest; otherwise, change will not be permanent or meaningful. If you have children of your own, extend the question: Would you want your own child to be a student in your room? How would they function under your current teaching style?

Look around your room. What does it signal? Can students move around freely, or is it all dictated by you? Can furniture be moved around, or is it enough to tell students that they may sit wherever they like? I go into more detail about what our classrooms signal in Chapter 4.

Film yourself teaching. I did this, albeit not for this purpose. The results were educational to say the least. I talked too much and did not notice the student nodding off, another student poking a neighbor with his pencil, and many other students squirming in their seats. It was clear to me by watching the tape that they were not listening, and yet in the moment I had not noticed. I had been too focused on getting to the point of the lesson.

So set up a video camera and let it record. It doesn't matter what lesson you are doing, just be prepared to critique yourself honestly.

Have students time you. I have done this to hilarious yet telling results. I ask the students to tell me when my time is up—so they set the timer for 10 minutes, and when it goes off, I am done talking. They have to hold me to it as well. The students feel in control, and I learn to get to the point faster and more efficiently. We then do something else, student-suggested or at the very least interactive, and later I am allowed to speak again for another 10 minutes if I need to, yet most days I have discovered that our mini-lesson, the foundation that they need to explore, can be covered within the 10 minutes. The students know that I expect full attention so that they can work the rest of the time. On those days where I need more time, I tell the students upfront that I will be speaking for a longer time and why. I treat them the same way I would an audience of adults because they deserve to know our purpose. Even the most tired elementary or middle school students will perk up if they know there is an end to the speaking coming. Extreme, perhaps, but it forces me to realize that I cannot drone on without having the students lose interest. The students know to pay very close attention while I do speak because soon they will be released to explore on their own.

Give them time to be experts. I had never taken the time to figure out who knew what in my room, so I did not know that I had a civil war expert, a geology expert, or a water-color expert hidden away. If you take the time to find out what your students are passionate about, you can then facilitate opportunities for them to share their expertise. This has come

> If you take the time to find out what your students are passionate about, you can then facilitate opportunities for them to share their expertise.

in handy for me many times as I have looked for students to take the lead on various projects. The easiest way for me to figure out expertise has been to have conversations with the students, however, now teaching middle school where our 45-minute classes do not allow for much free time, I have found blogging to be my preferred tool for uncovering student interests and expertise. Students blog bi-weekly on a range of topics and I pay attention as I approve their posts. Staff from my school also visit their blogs and in turn get to discover who our new students are as well. I also believe in the power of a great survey. Students want us to know more about them, so on the first day of school I offer them an opportunity to tell me more about themselves. I refer to this throughout the year as I start to connect the dots with what they have told me and what I see in front of me. I make it a point to know them as human beings and not just a member of a class.

Stop answering all of their questions (or at least some of them). Not answering student questions can be just as helpful as answering them, if not even more helpful. Not only will this signal your new role as facilitator rather than supreme knowledge giver, it will also encourage students to develop strategies to learn without you. What a gift that is! When we become adults, it's something we must be able to do as we self-direct our personal and professional growth. Yet, how do you do this without sounding like you just do not want to answer? Relationship and tone is vital. I ask a question back rather than refuse an answer, so if a student asks me an answer for something, I might ask them, "How will you find out?" The first time they inevitably will say by asking a teacher, which then prompts the follow-up question from me, "How else can you find out?" Students quickly catch on and start to problem-solve either by themselves or with a classmate to find the needed solution. Now, I do not do this for every single question, but I do it for many, even for those we seem to get every day: When is this due? Do you have a pencil? Where is this sheet? And so on. My principal pointed out to me how she could see that students were becoming self-sufficient since during an observation when a student asked when something was due, another student pointed to the board for the answer. I was no longer the only person with the knowledge, and that is a great thing.

Have a frank conversation with your students. While this requires quite a trusting community, admitting our mistakes as teachers is one memorable way to get all of us on the path to a new kind of classroom. I have told my students what I did not like about my classroom or teaching in a round-circle meeting and then asked them their opinion. Usually, only one or two students will share at first, so your reaction is key—thank them and ask further questions but withhold all judgment. They want to share their honest answers with you, but they will not if they are going to get punished for it. I also believe in a honesty policy that may be extreme: if I go home thinking a lesson was a flop I typically mention it to the students the next day, not so I can reteach it, but rather so they can tell me what went wrong. I have had more student buy-in because of my willingness to admit that I am not a perfect teacher, but instead someone who is trying to create the best possible learning environment, from my fourth graders and from my seventh graders. These conversations do not take up much time—but even if they did, the long-term investment in community and the pushback on my teaching is completely worth it.

Be open to feedback. Yes, coming from kids, the feedback may be pretty critical. Being told that your lessons are boring is never easy, but it certainly does make you think about what you are doing as a teacher. If students are willing to share their honest opinion, then please be open to listening to it without getting defensive. After all, this is a learning opportunity for them and for you. I am often asked when feedback should be solicited, but the truth is, it depends. I always start the year off with a big survey; I ask them for their honesty so that I can be the best teacher possible for them. The survey asks questions not just about their reading and writing habits, but also who they are as people. What are their fears and dreams? We start this on the first day of school, which lets the students know right away that I want to know more about them and that their answers matter to me. Throughout the year feedback is solicited when we start a unit to help me infuse their ideas into it and always at the end of something we have worked on for an extended period of time. This is the chance I need to hear what needs to be changed from a student perspective and not just what I have seen needs to change. Often this type of feedback is gathered through electronic or paper survey. Students can do them anonymously if they choose but most do not. Yet, feedback can be given in short conversations as well. It does not always have to be something meticulously planned for, but can be a brief conversation to start class. What matters most about feedback is that we ask for, listen to, and then act upon it. How we get it depends on how we operate.

Don't stop asking yourself the hard questions. Every year I reevaluate: Would I still like being a student in my classroom, or have I slipped backwards? Would I want my own child to be a part of this classroom? I also keep in mind the makeup of my students and their specific learning needs, then I adapt my room to fit their needs. Every year, I vow that this will be the year I figure it all out—and while that has yet to happen, it is vital that you trust in yourself and your ability to create a better environment for all of the learners who come to us. Keep pushing yourself forward so that you do not become stuck in a new routine, even if it is a better one. Our students change every year and so should our approach. Much like you are holding on to the things that have worked well in the past, hold on to some of the new, but explore further every year. Just because something is a better way does not make it the best way.

Give it time. Change can happen quickly, but it may not produce the results you were hoping for right away. Students have long been taught how to "do" school. For us, all of a sudden, to ask them to change how they are as learners can be startling. The shift requires time and commitment from you and all of the students. Start with small changes. Remember, progress is progress, no matter how small.

> Start with small changes. Remember, progress is progress, no matter how small.

Take a Breather!

Go ahead—close this book! Or at least feel free to put it down whenever you want. This book is meant to make you reflect and find things you can change.

So please do not feel the need to read it all at once, but instead take the time to read it in whichever way makes sense to you. That can mean jumping around in chapters or skipping entire sections. Use it the way that will be most beneficial to you—this is after all *your* learning journey. Also, not every idea presented in this book may make sense for you; that is perfectly alright. This book is not meant to be another expert book telling you how to teach but rather a book that inspires you to change in a way that works for you and your students. Do not lose yourself in the change; after all, you are the reason you became a teacher. To help you start your reflection, take a moment to fill out the reflection sheet in the appendix (page 158).

So You Got the Job. Now What?

"My advice for new teachers is to not take it extremely easy on us because they may be new but we are not." —Kiley J.

We've all been there (or perhaps you are still dreaming of being there)—arms full of papers, books falling out of bags, and so many questions as we enter our new job and first classroom that we hardly know what to ask or where to start.

The plight of a new teacher is frightening, indeed. Or perhaps you are a teacher switching grade levels or schools or districts. Whichever, when we move out of our comfort zone, we wonder whom we will turn to, and where we will find the elusive answers that can help us sleep better at night, before the big show. But which answers do we really need?

Then: Maybe I Could Sort of Change the World?

"My advice for new teachers is to be fun yet stern. Make sure there are some fun days and to mix it up."

—Connor F.

I think most teachers get into this job because they think they can make a difference, and many do. Yet as a new teacher both when I had never taught, but also when I switched districts and grade levels, the responsibility of my new classroom and the role of custodian for the dreams of my students was a crushing weight. Sure, I had people I could speak to about it all, but I still felt overwhelmed. I thought I had many of the answers—remember, Harry Wong and I had figured things out in the short summer before my first 19 students arrived. And yet, that nagging feeling that perhaps I really had no idea what I was doing haunted my own dreams.

So I went to work, listening to every piece of advice I could scrounge up—but those who have tried that approach can attest that it often just leaves you with more questions. I finally settled in with a notion of doing it by the book because I had no other way of doing it. I certainly did not think to reach out more to others, establish a Personal Learning Network (PLN), or even listen more to myself.

I believed that being new meant I had to follow someone else's advice for the first six weeks of school, or I would be doomed. Now I know that students mostly know how to do school, and we must respect their intelligence as we build community with them. (For more ideas on how to build community by giving students a voice, read my blog post at http://smartblogs.com/education/2013/06/21/how-to-give-students-a-voice-in-their-education.)

That very first year I thought I started out right. I had made connections with my new colleagues, who were warm and welcoming. I had set up my room just so, thinking it accurately reflected me as a person and definitely defined for the students who was in charge. I had come up with my very own rewards system: pizza parties for those who did not find themselves inscribed in my Book of Names. I had created a board called "The Awesome Board" where ⟨...⟩ ⟨disp⟩layed. I had laminated my pur⟨...⟩ ⟨d⟩irections.

The room ⟨...⟩ whiteboard where I would have ⟨...⟩ ⟨...⟩ve. And I believed the myths, the ⟨...⟩ ⟨pro⟩fessors and advice columnists. T⟨...⟩ ⟨...⟩-teacher books or passed down ⟨...⟩

This is cool!

Because my class gets very loud and excited about learning – I shouldn't stop that excitement. ↓

Now: My Stu⟨dent⟩

"I wish teachers ⟨...⟩ ⟨...⟩ time."—Aliya M.

Behold the te⟨...⟩ ⟨...⟩ the realities I now believe to be t⟨rue⟩

Myth 1: Children are only learning when they are quiet and focused on the teacher.

Reality: So we all know this isn't true, right? Well, I didn't, at least not the first two years. I thought if students were too noisy they couldn't hear the most important person in the room, me. I came to find out, it is often through these "disruptive" student conversations that deeper learning takes place. Yet, there needs also to be room for contemplation and reflection. We aim for a healthy balance of both within our classroom, depending on the task. Balance is key so simply put: get out of the way of learning.

Myth 2: As a new teacher, you should never send a student to the principal's office because it shows weakness and inexperience.

Reality: Your principals are your liaisons, so use them if needed. Realize, though, that when you do send a student to the office, the outcome of the situation is no longer your choice, so if you want to have a hand in it then engage the principal in a conversation with the child, rather than just doing a referral. Make it clear to students that going to the principal's office is to give them space, time to think, not to be punished.

Myth 3: Try to never ask for help, but if you must, do so in private.

Reality: Always ask for help, big or small. My first year, I was petrified that people would think my hiring was a mistake because I did not have all of the answers. Well, guess what? No one has all of the answers. When you approach someone and ask for help, you are showing trust, and through trust you build community. That sense of community can carry you through many situations and years of teaching. And do not stop asking just because you have been there a few years either: every year new challenges face us, so ask the questions that will help you face them.

Hopefully, someday you will be the one whom new teachers come to for help. And don't just ask for help within your school; get on Twitter and get involved with the thriving teacher community there. In fact, the sidebar below this chapter discusses how to get on Twitter without becoming overwhelmed.

I have read so many posts on how to get on Twitter and get connected. Many of them offer fantastic advice and yet some of them keep reiterating how it is all about following. Follow one person, and then see who they follow, and then follow them, and soon you will be following so many people you will feel like the most popular kid in the school. Except you don't. Instead you feel like the kid who came to the prom only to take pictures of all the cool people there. So I offer up these tips instead for those trying to figure out Twitter.

1. **Follow one person, or even 10, but then stop.** Let yourself process what Twitter is and how these people are using the tool. Don't mass follow. You will find enough people to follow, just take your time.

2. **Connect.** Once you have a couple of people you follow, reach out to them. Tell them you are new, tell them your story, and comment on their blogs. Open up about yourself, start a conversation, and give them a reason to connect back.

3. **Don't give up.** Sometimes I felt like the biggest loser when it came to Twitter; no one thought I was witty, no one RTed my posts, until I realized that this is not what Twitter is about. Twitter is about the connections (I know, I sound like a broken record), so it is not about the retweets or single comments but the dialogue you get involved in and the people you meet.

4. **Who cares about klout?** I didn't realize I had a klout number until my husband asked me what it was. Then I had to look it up because that little number meant nothing to me; it still doesn't. If you are asking whether Twitter is worth your time you probably haven't connected with the right people, so keep connecting.

5. **Don't worry about the popular kids.** One thing for ongoing discussion has been the grades of popularity Twitter educators seem to have. Sure, there are people with massive followings—but guess what? They are normal people and they probably have that many followers because they say some really great things and they are good at connecting with others. It is okay to reach out to them as well; no one is off limits.

6. **Make it work for you.** Twitter is what Twitter does. I constantly use Twitter in new ways that work for me. For Twitter to truly become a useful tool for you, it has to fit your needs. There is no wrong or right way to use it (although there may be better or worse ways).

So there you have it, my small piece of advice on how to get something out of Twitter. Of course, you can follow as many people as you want, but think about what your true goal is: numbers or connections? I, for one, count my connections just as much as I count my blessings.

Myth 4: Listen, but do not talk, during staff meetings.

Reality: I am a perpetual hand-raiser (there, I admit it). I am also guilty of thinking aloud and most likely having an opinion. While I do not recommend turning staff meetings into your one-person show, if you have a question, or perhaps even an opinion, please share it. You may be surprised by the discussion that ensues because of something you said. Successful staff meetings rely on discussion, so become a partner in that, not just a fly on the wall. It is okay for you to have a voice in your very first year.

Myth 5: Take a break from school/professional development your first year since you will be so busy.

Reality: I know college is hard. I worked almost full-time while I went to school full-time. It was tough! The first year of teaching is even tougher, but that does not mean you should stop learning. Check out the professional development offered in your area or online, or better yet create a PLN so that whenever you have time, you can be engaged in conversation with educators from all over the world. Model for your students what a true lifelong learner looks like by becoming one yourself.

Myth 6: Show up at all extracurricular activities your students participate in.

Reality: I know students love to see us outside of school, and I love to see my students participating in something they are passionate about, but it is okay to say no once in a while. With all the piano recitals, dance performances, football games, and basketball tournaments, I hardly ever saw my husband, my family, or my friends. So pick a couple of general events. I always go to whatever my school puts on and see almost all of my kids in one swoop. Now that I have children of my own, I bring them along, which makes for an even more exciting meetup for my students. If you attend one student's solo event then you will feel obligated to go to as many as possible—and that can be exhausting if you have a large class size. So yes, they love to see you out in the real world, but don't forget to attend to your own life. After all, that's what makes you interesting!

Myth 7: Work through your breaks to show you are serious.

Reality: There is nothing more serious than a first-year teacher—always rushing about, eating lunch in the hallway while running to the copier, or stealing a snack while he or she helps students during lunch. I did it, and I still do sometimes, but give up your breaks in moderation. Going to the teacher's lounge may seem like a silly event, or perhaps you have been warned that it is nothing but a room for burned-out teachers to spew their negativity. Actually, the

> Don't be afraid to try new things, even if it is your first year. After all, you are trying to discover who you are as a teacher, not just becoming a really good copy of someone else.

teacher's lounge or being in the company of other professionals is where I have had some of my most meaningful conversations and also developed friendships with other teachers. I always have kids who hate going out to recess or need help with homework. Yet it is okay to say no sometimes and let them know they should take their break as well.

Myth 8: Don't try t   th in a a

Reality: I am an ic   es and get so
excited to   st. Yet I was
told repea   all, this was
my first y   f my "crazy"
ideas, and   ed for others,
but not fc   y new things,
even if it   g to discover
who you   good copy of
someone   ng to try, but
do try so   ne to uncover
who you   r to start that
explorati

> *Don't be afraid to try new things! Don't always go by the book.*

Myth 9: Model/s   idents to do.

Reality: I am no   g. But I have
found that often students like a challenge. Instead of showing them the whole process, try telling them the goal, give them a beginning, and let them discover. Learning is, after all, about the journey of discovery and not just the end of the trip. Trust them to try things and fail and watch them grow as independent learners. If this scares you, start with a small project and give students some freedom there.

Myth 10: You must be/act happy at all times, or the "Go in there and win the Oscar" myth.

Reality: Students respond to humanness, and, in particular, genuine human beings. While I do not recommend teaching in a foul mood, it is okay to lower the pitch, as long as you explain why this is. The explanation, of course, depends on the grade level you teach.

When my grandfather died, I found out an hour before I had to be at school. This man had influenced me in more ways than I can count, and his passing was one of deep sorrow for me and the rest of my family. Yet I showed up at school, told my students, and my students embraced me and carried me through the day, knowing that I had chosen to be with them in a moment that was so deeply personal. This is how meaningful connections are made. You show them that you care enough to trust them with your real life. Maybe they will trust you too.

Next: What You Can Do, Starting Today

Whenever a new year approaches, I always get so excited. More school! It beckons me with the possibility of great connections and deep exploration. I think back to that first year and what I wish I had done instead. Perhaps my yearnings for a fresh start will help inspire you to do things your way very early on or help you if you are experiencing a new start later in your career.

Reach out! Remember that interview team you sat across from, trying to connect with? Well, now is the time to make the actual connection. So email them, find them on Twitter or Facebook, Google them—do something and reach out. Set up a time to meet, whether formally or informally. Don't wait until the first day of school; there will be so many others to connect with at that point.

Ask questions. When you reach out, ask questions about curriculum, ask questions about school quirks. Truly there is no such thing as a dumb question in this situation. I still remember my long list and just how gracious my team members were to me.

Ask for resources. Do not reinvent the wheel. I created so much of my own stuff that first summer, only to find out my team already had much of it made, often better than my own. Bring your ideas to the table but also ask to use some of theirs. There will be plenty of tasks to do on your own. Again, this is where an online PLN can be incredibly handy, so take it beyond Google and swap ideas through Twitter and other networking tools.

Do your homework. Discover whatever you can on your own, first. Things like math curriculum and other major district decisions can probably be found through a quick website search. That way you can save your 911 calls for those things that are a little more complicated.

Find out about necessary PD classes. Again, this may be something a teammate tells you, but see if there are classes you need to take. Every year districts seem to implement some new program or approach, and new teammates only know this if they are told. So in case someone forgets to tell you, do the research, and then sign up for the classes. You do not want to start the year already behind in professional development.

Reflect. Now that you have the job, what is your primary goal for your first year? (And please don't say survival—teaching shouldn't be about surviving but about thriving!) What do you hope to pass on to all of those kids, your teammates, your school, and yourself? Where do you want to see yourself next year? Make a tentative plan for what type of teacher you would like to be and work toward it, be ready to modify or abandon it if need be, but start out with a dream at least.

Stop with the extreme prep work. I made so many copies and spent so much time laminating everything my first year. Why? I am not sure. It felt like a full-time job sometimes, but I was so sure that everything needed to be protected and copied. Crazy, really. So figure out what is important to you, take stock of what you will be doing in your prep time, and ask yourself, "Does my supply list really need to be laminated?"

Enjoy! There is no time like the one you are in, all fresh and ready for those first students. So get yourself psyched up, because Year One is truly a memorable experience. Allow yourself to trust yourself. Allow yourself to feel like you have something valuable to add. And finally, allow yourself to be just a little bit freaked out. You cannot prepare for everything, but you got the job because yo[u]

And for all of y[ou] chose to start anew later in your [who] begin a new and often frighteni[ng]

Be fearless. I k[now] here the kids won't quiet down screaming at them just to take a[t] e. It may feel that way at times, op of a table t for bad rea- although the y, it will also e for you to ts you teach. connections, or a common vision. How often do we get to say that we get to start over again and really mean it?

So have goals. Be brave. It is okay to present new ideas that you might not have thought out completely, but that you know in your stomach will probably work. It is okay to try something and then have it fail. It is okay to not have every answer. It is okay to show the

> Realize that although the next year will be filled wi[th] scary, it will also be filled with new. A new chance f[or] you to spread your passic[on] for the subjects you teach. A new chance for you to build connections, to be a part of a team, to work for a common vision. How often do we get to say that we get to start over again and really mean it?

Handwritten notes:
- Trust yourself
- Feel that you have something valuable to add.
- Be just a little freaked out

students that you are nervous like them, too. It is okay to let your inner dork shin as long as you embrace it as a strength.

Be true to you. You have a vision f so make it work—but not just for you, l you with their curiosity, their fears, th your room, much like you hope to feel s words don't matter. Words matter mor will never be able to reach them all– you don't know who you are reaching of them; keep trying for all of them. Ev possibly push you any harder.

Don't lose yourself in the job. Yes, t is this all-consuming amazing experiei we can live and breathe. But you are only as good of a teacher as you are a person outside of school. You may have kids at home who need their days listened to, their curiosity protected, who need time with just you. Not you and your computer. Not you and your teaching ideas. So give yourself fully when you are at school, but then leave it behind when you

> "you will never be able to reach them all ... you don't know who you are reaching at what time."

> them all—but the trick with teaching is that you don't know who you are reaching at what time. So don't give up on any of them; keep trying for all of them.

drive home; allow your brain to rest and your soul to be nourished. You are a better teacher when you have a life you love outside of school.

Say yes to as much as you can. Say yes to that that scares you. We only grow when we push ourselves. But don't say yes so much that you cannot find the time to breathe. There may be more opportunities than ever coming your way and so many things you would like to do. But just don't. Allow yourself the luxury of saying "No, thank you"; allow yourself the luxury of not volunteering for everything. Embrace the life you have and say yes to the things that matter the most.

Don't be ashamed of being you. You may not always have the best advice. You may not always be an expert. You may not always know what you are doing, but you still have worth. Your ideas still matter. You still matter. Your excitement can spread. Your newness may be an advantage at times. Your energy and curiosity will help you. So don't stand in your own way.

A new year will always be an adventure—you already know that—but a new year is just another year. Even on your worst days, it will only be a day. The tide will always turn. There will always be more good than bad. More success than failure. You can only do your best; you can only bring everything you've got; you can only do so much. There will be much outside of your control, but how you feel about it is in your hands: don't forget that. Smile, laugh, think, reflect, reach out, be you, be kind, be honest, wonder, and try. Yes, a new job when we have grown so comfortable in our old will be scary at first, but anything amazing always is. I have a feeling it will be just fine, you just have to believe it yourself.

4

It's Not How Your Classroom Looks, It's How It Feels

"A classroom should be set up to where students always have the opportunity to say whatever they want as long as it's on topic."

—Isabel O.

During my college studies of classroom management, a visiting elementary teacher told us: ". . . and if you walk into our room you may be surprised at the noise and the mess, but to me that means the students are engaged." I was horrified.

Noise? Mess? Not this teacher! How could anyone possibly learn in noise or out of their desks? I was going to run my classroom like a machine. I cringe now at that memory. I look around my classroom, thinking back to that elementary teacher's comment, and realize we *are* that room! We're the class you can hear coming down the hallway, the one where students are splayed out on the floor, discussing, laughing, and, gosh golly, sharpening their pencils whenever they like. Yet, we are also the room where students are so quietly focused on their books or writing that it's almost eerie, who groan when I tell them time is up and class is almost over, who have a purpose and enough sense to know we have to get to work and therefore stay mostly focused. We are a room that changes with our learning, and that change often comes from the students.

There are no laminated rules posters (other than the district-mandated one filled in by the students and hung on a wall), no reminders of how to get your stuff done or how to enter into the classroom, no sticks to move or stars to give and receive. We don't need those things in a learning space being run with and by the students.

It's a classroom in which we all have our rightful place, and our routines change based on our needs of the moment. To the untrained eye it may seem chaotic at times—after all, students crave routines—but if you look closer you will notice the patterns of established behavior expectations are there. Students get to work, and they stay focused; they treat each other with respect; they take care of the physical space and know that it is their room. Yes, even in my seventh grade classroom.

I wish this had been my classroom the first few years of my teaching career—a place shared by all of us and not just Mrs. Ripp's space. Instead, my room felt like a Marine barrack, and me a slightly kinder drill sergeant. I dictated how we walked down the hallway, how we got our jackets and backpacks, how we acted when others came into the classroom, how we borrowed books from the library, how we asked for supplies. Don't answer the phone; don't sit in my chair; don't eat your food now. Don't, don't, don't.

Everything had a protocol. I was so busy keeping track of all my check-out sheets and reminders that I forgot to just enjoy what I was doing with the students. I was so wrapped up in managing my space that I lost focus on what was important in that space: the students. Instead I wasted time getting upset when my system wasn't followed. It was time-consuming, overcomplicated, and downright ridiculous.

I don't imagine there are many new teachers who achieve a sense of shared classroom ownership in their first years. It requires a deep level of trusting yourself as a teacher and facilitator. But I certainly think it's possible to begin your career with the best kind of classroom. I simply never had anyone encouraging me to trust my instincts and not the well-meaning advice of "experts."

So here it is: **trust yourself!** Whether you are a new teacher or one who's more experienced but stuck in a traditional place, the most important thing for you to do is figure out who *you* are. Pursue what you believe are the best teaching practices—then start to question them as part of your regular reflection.

Of course you will change stuff as you go along—modifying this, rejecting that. But you will be using your own judgment to shape your evolution as a teacher. You will decide what outside advice is worth listening to as you and your students shape the teaching and learning space.

Now: This Is Our Room, Our World

"Kids should be able to sit where they want in the room and have a say in moving things such as desks and chairs."

—Jumana T.

I once believed that the classroom had to revolve around my needs and that students were temporary visitors granted gracious permission to exist in my universe. Now I believe that the room is theirs and that they own it as much as I do.

In the early years, I reduced the possibilities down to two: my contrived systems, or chaos. My fear of chaos fed the growth of my control systems, to the point where I got so lost I didn't know the teacher I was anymore. So I stopped the endless control.

I "let" students borrow books from my library and take them home. Yes, I may lose more books but I also do not spend hours trying to manage a library with more than hundreds of titles in it. I show the students where I keep all of the supplies and let them grab what they want. When I taught elementary, students would unpack and enter the classroom in a way that suited them best: some needed one trip, some needed more. I stopped obsessing over systems and started emphasizing choices.

And the result? Not chaos as I had feared, but ownership. It turned out that these students knew exactly how to take care of our space and actually were a lot more invested in the learning real estate when they felt it was theirs. They no longer ask permission to use a stapler or some tape, they just do it. They fight me over my chair and take pencils when they need them. They welcome others to our room, answer the phone with their name, and commandeer space when they need it. I don't manage them but instead focus on our learning and help them build the skills they need as responsible human beings.

Giving the classroom back to your students is more than just changing one's mindset; it is also about physically changing the room to signal the change. The teacher's desk, the flow patterns, even what is on your walls all mirror the expectations of the classroom. I'm always asking myself: <u>does the space allow the students to belong?</u>

With every year, and with every room move or even school move, I cannot help but

> Giving the classroom back to your students is more than just changing one's mindset; it is also about physically changing the room to signal the change. The teacher's desk, the flow patterns, even what is on your walls all mirror the expectations of the classroom.

dream of what is to come. I think it is one of the most magical things about being a teacher—the "what will happen?" of the new year. Therefore, every year, I ask myself these questions:

To desk or not to desk? I was offered the granddaddy of teacher desks one year: huge, sleek, brand new. I turned it down gladly. Several years ago, I decided to go deskless, and I have never looked back. Instead, I have a table for my computer and planner but it is tucked into the corner where I don't get drawn behind it, isolating myself from the kids.

Tables or desks? I have had both small desks and large tables. While I have loved having large tables for the ease of collaboration and movement, this year going back to small moveable desks in the middle school has proven to be quite beneficial for my students. Every class comes in and quickly arranges the desks in the way they see fit for our purpose. Some prefer to group themselves in a larger group of students for discussion while others like to pull a few desks aside for a more intimate conversation. The students know they can move them as they see fit and little time is wasted on it. Rarely do I ask them to leave the desks in place and I can tell by this simple measure of trust they have taken more ownership over the room. They make it work for their needs, not fit their needs around our room.

What is on our walls? I used to plaster my walls with *those posters* where the brightly colored animals are saying cute motivational things. My theory? Wherever you looked you would be motivated to hang in there, work hard, and make great decisions. I took them down five years ago. Now, when the school year begins I have very few things hanging on our walls—this year it was only a world map and a comic. Everything else we add as we go. I asked one group of students what they thought about the motivational posters, and one replied: "Oh those. I always start to read those whenever I am bored." If I had ever needed more reason to remove them, her honest response had just handed it to me.

Are you in the room? My students become part of my family, so I have framed pictures of my family, as well as weekly drawings from my oldest daughter for the classroom. I also happen to be a comic-book lover and so a few pieces of comic book art hang on our walls as well. The pieces that I hang are intentional and make me happy. The students often ask questions about the pictures, but I don't take over the room. I don't need a room that feels like *my* room. I need a room that will welcome in any child, even if I don't teach them. So I purposefully do not overdecorate, nor have a theme—unless you can count an obsession for books as my theme. I do not ever want a child to feel excluded from a room because there was no room for their personality to be a part of it.

Which way do your desks face? My former students told me they didn't want to face the Smartboard but rather the whiteboard because we used that much more. So this year that is exactly how they face. However, once again, the students can move about as they like, so in all honesty I am not too bothered by how they face. I don't need to be the center of attention, so the desks don't need to face me either. Allowing student ownership over such small things can make a bigger difference than we think, particularly if you teach in a school where students do not have a homeroom. Students still need to feel at home and they won't be able to if they cannot leave their mark on our classrooms, even if it means something as simple as being able to move furniture around.

Other areas? Are there places for the students to work that don't include their desks? I have bean bags, carpet squares, and small pillows that students use to get more comfortable. I have dreams for more moveable furniture and more spaces for them to work, but we work with what we have. I don't ask questions as to how students use the extra things we have in the room; if they need them, they use them. In fact, when I asked my students what they wanted in a perfect classroom, most of them answered extra places to work that were not their tables. So I make sure there is space for them to work that is away from their desk, such as providing them with access to clipboards, lap desks, and other surfaces to use. This is easy for us to do.

Can students get what they need? I used to hide all of my extra supplies and would get really upset if students dared ask for a pencil. Now, I have bins of stuff they may need, which they can grab, and they know to just ask if they need something that isn't out. My goodness, who hasn't ever needed an eraser? Pencils are a hot commodity as well and so those are easily accessible. Yet, I don't mean just easy access within the classroom, but also after they leave. My students know they can come at any time to borrow a book, snag a pencil, grab a clipboard, or leave me a note. If I am teaching, they walk in quietly, take care of what they need to do, and then leave, no harm done. The final layer of access becomes the online access we can provide students with to help them navigate our classroom. I have had a classroom blog for more than five years, which serves as a hub for parents and the world to get a glimpse into our room, but also allows students access to any materials or handouts we have used in class. Students know from the very first day that if they go to mrsripp.com, chances are that whatever they need can be found there.

Where are those rules? Anyone who walks in will notice there is no class constitution, no rules, no "what happens when . . ." posters in our room. Expectations are discussed by the students and changed as needed. With only 20% of the walls available for use due to fire code, I am not wasting any space on rules.

Where's the tech? I am fortunate to work in a BYOD district, which means most students have a device, but it also means most students have access to different functions. Some students carry a smart phone, while others have Chromebooks or tablets. I encourage students to bring their device every day to class in case we need it and also to use the Chromebooks that we have available to us as a team. If students need other tools, we try to find them for them; they know to grab what they need when we have it. Trusting students with technology is part of building a trusting community. They know how expensive the tools are, they know how to take care of them, so I let them prove it to me every single day.

Next: What You Can Do, Starting Today

"It should look and feel like a safe and fun place to learn in."—Emily S.

Whether you are a new teacher or a veteran, there are things that you can do right away to change the feel of your classroom. Pick and choose those that make sense to you and come up with your own as well. My list of questions is merely a start.

> Whether you are a new teacher or a veteran, there are things that you can do right away to change the feel of your classroom. Pick and choose those that make sense to you and come up with your own as well.

Which way does your desk face? Or do you even have a desk? Think of what your desk signals. Are you trying to create a barrier between you and the kids? What other purpose does it serve? I faced my work table toward the wall so that I am not tempted to sit behind it, and so there is no distance between the students and me, and it works. Because of its location, it is not the first thing you see and I don't sit behind it. It has become a place for students to work, as long as they keep it clean. And they do not feel that if I call them up there to talk it is because they are in trouble.

What is on your bulletin boards? I used to be the master of fancy bulletin boards. I loved to express my inner artist, and I was very obsessive over my border and letter placement. Unfortunately, that meant that I had nowhere to showcase student work or things we needed to see throughout the year. My bulletin boards in elementary were not perfect by the end, but instead were functional, because I had handed the responsibility of maintenance over to my students. As the year progressed, a student bulletin board committee changes them as they see fit, a committee I did not invent but one that a few ingenious students came up with. They wanted to have a voice in what people saw as they approached our room and so they asked if they could take over all of the bulletin work. I agreed after discussing their ideas and never looked back; their displays did a far better job showcasing the type of classroom we were than anything I could ever have created. In my current middle school I do not have any outside bulletin boards but instead focus on the space we have within the classroom. I leave it blank when it is not needed and only post stuff we are using at the moment. Functionality once again trumps beauty: I have learned to let go of slightly crooked letters and borders that need one more staple to stay tight.

How much space does your teacher stuff take up? Is every space yours, or is it open for student use? Do you have so many things out that you may need more bins to keep it all contained? I try to keep my stuff in cabinets, leaving impromptu work areas for the kids. It sends the message that I am not the most important person—that this is our space, and they have as much claim to the counter tops and shelves as I do.

What do people see from the hallway? When people walk by what do they see? Tables? Your desk? Nothing? At the moment, when people walk by our room, they will see our tables, empty spaces, and framed pictures and quotes. This will obviously change as we change what we are doing at the moment, but what visitors see does influence how a classroom is viewed and contributes to the overall feel of the school.

What is the classroom flow like? Can students move, or will they constantly have to ask someone else to push a chair out of the way? This is often out of our hands, but we can work out the best overall flow before the students get there. Can kids access the high-frequency areas such as cabinets, supplies, reading corner, or will they have to squeeze by, take a strange route, or get stuck in random places? Can the students "breathe" in the room, or is it filled to the brim with all of your "treasures"? Ask the students and watch their patterns those first few weeks of school; I don't think a year has gone by where we haven't changed something within the first few weeks.

Do they need permission? In my first year, I was totally obsessed with keeping things in their place. If that particular reading chair belonged in the reading corner, then that is where it belonged; no permissions to move it were granted. Now students take the movable furniture wherever they need it, and at the end of the day we put it all out of the way. Back in my drill sergeant days, I even dictated their desk supplies. I told them exactly what they had to have in their pencil cups (no, seriously I did), and then patrolled to see if they followed my orders. Now they put what they want in their cups and tuck them away whenever they don't need them.

What else do you need to physically change to signify the philosophical change you are experiencing? My list of suggestions is just that; a place to get started with. Do not let it limit you. The best place to start if you are not sure how to approach your classroom redesign is once again the students and creating a venue for them to have shared ownership over the environment. That does not mean that your views and ideas should be removed from the overall feel of the room, but that your ideas should work alongside with those of the students. While this may seem easier to do in a single classroom setting such as the ones we see in fourth or fifth grade, I have found this to also work in my current job as a middle school teacher. I may have more than 100 students who use my room every single day but because we have small desks rather than tables they can easily adapt their surroundings to fit their needs. And so while I dream of beautiful new furniture that would include all types of workspaces for students, I make things work with what I have: old desks, small tables, an assortment of bookcases and some beat-up bean bags. It is not so much what we put into our room physically but rather how our room feels to those that use it. And right now our room invites students to come in, find a book, and start to read.

5

The First Day of School: Who's In Charge?

"Don't just teach us it, we won't listen, so do something that will make it stick more in our brains." —Carlie M.

No teacher begins a teaching career with ill intentions. Yet most of us make our biggest mistake during our very first days in the classroom, whether we are brand-new or veteran teachers. I was no different, six years ago. I chose to do everything the way I saw others doing it, rather than explore how I felt it needed to be done. Once I had cemented what to do I never veered off that chosen path; after all, if I could only figure out the best way to control the students, then my teaching would be a success.

Then: Don't Smile Until December

"How can teachers make learning more interesting? Be more fun, make jokes, and smile."

—Carson K.

Sure, I laughed with the students and made noises about our "class community." But as the all-important first week of school progressed, I went about dictating rules, establishing who was in control, and setting tight boundaries for the year. As a result, I lost the opportunity to create the kind of relationship with my students that leads not only to motivation and engagement but to real ownership of learning and ultimately greater achievement.

I made my very first misstep on orientation day. I was so nervous meeting all of the parents that I barely focused on the students. It was those parents

I wanted to impress, particularly since this was my first year, and I did not want any parent to feel their child might be at a disadvantage by being with the new teacher. The day went smoothly, with no hard questions. I remember thinking I must have passed the test.

The very next day, I stood eagerly by my door shaking the hands of all of the fourth grade students entering my room. I had already laid out activities for them to do, and I was eager to start our very first conversation about how to enter the classroom. As all of the students took their assigned seats, I asked them for their attention and then proceeded to show them exactly how I wanted them to enter the room, what they needed, and what the consequences would be for entering unprepared. Students nodded along.

We moved on to the next important conversation: my rules, and the consequences for breaking them. Here is where I relied on another new-teacher staple, *The First Six Weeks of School* by Paula Denton and Roxann Kriete. The authors pose the enticing idea of making it appear that your students themselves are coming up with the classroom rules and procedures, thus facilitating buy-in as you steer them to the inevitable conclusion. In fact, I had the rules typed up in advance: "Respect each other, take care of yourself, and take care of our property."

My intentions were noble. I wanted my students to feel like they were part of the management of the classroom. But I was creating a false notion. I had no intention of letting them set the rules. I knew from all my training and reading that my number-one job was to be the leader of this learning space. And leaders make the rules.

The rest of that first week of school was an actual blur. Most teachers (veteran and new) are dazed by the end of the first week, caught up in the anxiousness to get started with curriculum, but also busy figuring out who their students are and how they will manage them throughout the year. And can we forget just how exhausted we are? I was in awe of the kindness my kids had shown to me, but also very tightly gripping the reins of control for all of our learning. Now was not the time to appear too weak or too friendly.

I'd staged numerous ice-breaking activities, and I thought we had gotten to know each other well. In fact, I knew very little about each student, definitely not anything that could guide me in my teaching. I didn't know who their favorite author was, what they struggled with, or what their expectations for fourth grade were. I figured those things would come later (and sometimes they did), but in reality I had completely missed the biggest opportunity I would have to truly get to know my students.

In essence, I was fearful that if I did not firmly assert my authority from the very first day of school, the rest of the year would be out of control. So assert I did—that year and for several years after. We did okay. I taught. My students learned. But I could sense so much wasted potential beneath my iron grip.

Now: What I Can't Wait to Do the First Week!

"How can teachers make learning more fun? By getting advice from the students."
—Athena R.

Now I know that what we do in the first week of school through communication, listening, and genuine interest sets the tone for the rest of the year more deliberately than any set of rules or expectations ever will. I have also realized that while the first day is important (first impressions always are), it is really what comes after that matters most.

Students expect an exciting first day or at the very least a day that makes them feel welcome. They are often nervous and filled with energy, ready to see their friends, ready to hear what the year will hold, ready to meet their teacher. That energy bubbles into a classroom and sustains it for a day. We do fun things, we set the tone, we explain and explore, and I always end with a challenge. At the end of the day, I am exhausted and exhilarated, ready for an amazing year. And I hope my students go home and tell their parents that this year will be an incredible adventure.

Yet for me it is the next several days that set the true tenor for the year. When the initial excitement fades, it begins to dawn on the students that summer is over and school is back. Some have found that they are more nervous than they thought they would be. Some may even begin to realize that their teacher is not quite what they thought she or he would be, that first day of school. Some have decided that school will simply be more of what they already know and will therefore be ready to check out on us. This is when we start to make our lasting impression.

When we no longer have time to do the fun beginning-of-the year activities, when we start to feel the pressure of everything we have to get done, when students start to show their real personalities—that is when our students begin to discover who we really are and how we really will be as a teacher.

Anyone can fool kids for a day. But no one can fool kids for a whole year. So ask yourself: what are you doing the rest of the week? The rest of the month? The rest of the year? What comes after when the realities of another year of school has settled in and the students no longer are excited to come? That is where we should be focusing our efforts for a year of passionate learning.

As I look back at the first weeks of that very first year, I am amazed again at the resilience of 10-year-olds. Many of those students still tell me that our year together was their favorite year, while I wonder how I ever convinced them that I was doing right by them. I made so many mistakes, but they never lost their faith—they searched for the bright spots and simply trudged through all of the boring routine.

As I began to think seriously about change, I first called upon my expertise. I was now a master at setting up the first week of school to assert my authority and control. So I decided to imagine the blueprint for the worst possible school year, from a powerless student's point of view. Behold.

My Recipe for an Awful School Year

- **Step 1:** Start with that very first meeting. Lay down a big heaping helping of the Law. You are the teacher and have the degree to prove it.
- **Step 2:** Make sure they know their place. Label it. Carefully designate the area they can spread out—their desk or their assigned seat. Mark off your own territory by using the furniture provided. Think of it as a fortress to be penetrated only by the most fearless of students.
- **Step 3:** When they ask to go to the bathroom, tell them they will have to wait for the designated bathroom break time. Watch them squirm. After all, we adults have to learn how to hold it, and school is all about preparing students for the real world.
- **Step 4:** Dehydration is overrated. No water breaks until their designated bathroom breaks. Snacks are for recess; we do not need any crumbs to invade our learning space.
- **Step 5:** If they run out of school supplies, make it clear it's their job to get more. You are, after all, not an office supply store.
- **Step 6:** Books will be selected by you at all times and will be a direct reflection of their reading level. Mostly they will be about whatever the curriculum tells us we have to study. Who has the time to discuss interests with 20+ kids?
- **Step 7:** Homework is to be handed in before attendance is given, no exceptions. In the real world, one must learn to meet deadlines or suffer the consequences. Don't bother to suggest work that interests you for extra credit. Any extra credit will be determined by the teacher and will usually involve a task the teacher needs done.
- **Step 8:** Parents should only come when invited, which means the first day of school, for conferences, and the last day of school. They really have no place or say in your room.
- **Step 9:** Parent conferences will be held at designated times, and the main person speaking will be the teacher. Students must be present to defend themselves, if need be, but otherwise they will remain quiet and attentive.

- ◆ **Step 10:** No talking in the halls; whisper voices only at lunch. All eyes on the teacher after she flips the lights off and on repeatedly. No pencil sharpening outside the designated time window.
- ◆ **Step 11:** Include a test on the very first day—something to help figure out where the students' deficits are. As soon as this testing is done students can be placed in designated groups for the rest of the year. Make those first tests part of their grade to accurately measure their growth throughout the year.
- ◆ **Step 12:** Surprise them with tests early and often. It creates an aura of mystery around the teacher, and students will never know quite what to think.
- ◆ **Serving tips:** The less students know about you, the better. We are not here to build relationships, we are here to teach and to get them ready for the test. The children will address you properly by your correct title and last name. Keep your first name to yourself. You do not want them to be able to find you outside of school. Your personal life is completely private.

While my awful recipe is riddled with irony, I shudder at how many of these things I used to do. And what about now? If you come into my classroom on the very first day of school, you will see something very different—a kinder, slower, more open approach, in tune with what I believe the students really need: respect and a place to call their own. Oh, and lots of books to be read.

Cooking Up a Great Year

"How can teachers make learning fun? By letting us have some choice in what we do and freedom."

—Deja S.

Walk into our classroom that first week and you will see a community being built, not through random ice breakers (even though some of those can be used for a laugh), but through meaningful activities that start to shake us up together and make us trust each other. I now realize that if I take my time with my students during our first days together, it will pay off all the rest of the year. Here's my thinking:

- ◆ **We are all brand new to each other.** Yes, I may have had their sister, or I may have been with them before in a different capacity,

> To find common ground, I ask them about their lives, not just their summer. And I tell them, "Please don't hold back, don't be afraid to upset me." If they hate reading or school, I need to know that; otherwise, I will never be able to battle their demons.

but let's face it, we are all brand-new classmates on that first day of school, and we just want to be understood and to feel welcome. To find common ground, I ask them about their lives, not just their summer. And I tell them, "Please don't hold back, don't be afraid to upset me." If they hate reading or school, I need to know that; otherwise, I will never be able to battle their demons. This early communication is a seed, hopefully, for a relationship that will span the entire year and beyond.

◆ **We are cementing our routines.** I am not a fan of many prescriptive systems, but over the years my students and I have discovered certain routines that make our classroom work efficiently and effectively. So we discuss what they may be, and then we decide on a common way to describe them so that others may understand the routine as well. We also discuss why and when we need routines; sometimes, students know more than I give them credit for. Then we move on.

◆ **We are discovering our rules.** I don't set the rules in our classroom, my students (really) do. So we take the time within the first day or two to discuss what we want our room to sound like, feel like, and look like. What type of experience do we want this classroom to have? We have also created our vision for the year videos using Animoto so that we are reminded throughout the year of our lofty goals. We do not write the rules down but bring them up when needed throughout the year. This is such a vital component of my first week of class; the students need to know that their voice matters and that they play a powerful part in our room.

◆ **We look ahead.** The curriculum will mean nothing if we do not get excited about it. School has been done to children for so many years. I want to see them get excited about what this year of learning will mean for them. To do that you have to invest the time in exploring just what the year will look like. So we pull our curriculum a little apart, just so we know where we are headed and all the things we have to look forward to. However, we do not look too far into the future—this will mostly just waste time if we do, since students will not remember it anyway.

◆ **We relish our freedom.** I sometimes have to un-teach certain classroom behaviors because we work a little bit differently in this room. Instead of always raising a hand to answer, we work on how to have an "adult" discussion. We figure out how to work independently, where our help can come from, as well as how to take control of our misguided attempts or abject failures and figure out where to go from there. Students tend to think at first that I am trying to trick them into misbehaving. They have to see that I am not asking them to get in trouble, but rather to find themselves as learners. This takes time but is very important for the rest of the year.

◆ **We have to build trust.** Without trust, many of the things that we do—such as student blogging—will not work. I don't demand their trust or expect it blindly; I earn it just as they have to earn mine. Respect and representing ourselves well is something I hold very dear, and I try to pass those values on to my students. If we do not trust each other to learn together, if we do not trust each other to fail together, then we cannot overcome all of the challenges we need to conquer. Trust is the big ten

◆ **Finally, I want us to focus** *very first thing we do.* So inst first thing I do is read a pict picture book they choose, b books will be a central tenet up to my rocking chair—ye comfortable, and then share have the courage to share th I hope they have the courag "old," it is okay to think pic

[handwritten note: Trust each other to fail together/ learn together!]

Next: What You Can Do, Starting ?

"Teachers should do more activities, not like paperwork or sitting and talking, but activities where we students and even the teacher get up, move around, and bond with each other."

—Emily A.

There are many ways to start the first week of school. I recommend you start by skipping or doing very little of the following things and instead think about your hopes for the year:

Don't prepost your rules. Nothing says "This is my classroom" like a beautifully laminated poster of your rules that's been hanging there for years. Students will certainly know who the boss is the minute they enter and that they are, indeed, just visitors in your room.

Don't spend days writing a class constitution. As a social studies lesson, I think this might make be a marvelous project. But it's not a way to build classroom community. Think of it through the eyes of a child—days spent discussing the rules for the rest of the year and then pledging to uphold all 20 or so of them. What a dull way to start out together.

Don't "set clear boundaries" and label them. I was a label master, making sure students knew exactly when they had crossed into my territory, whether it be my desk, my cabinets, or my pencils. With labels come restrictions, and classrooms have enough restrictions put on them already; we do not need to add more.

Don't invest much time in icebreakers. I know some will disagree with me, but many adults will confess how much they hate icebreakers; why should students be any different? They make many people feel incredibly uncomfortable. Instead, invest the time in something meaningful as a community, such as a connections map, or a student-designed tour of the classroom, or anything that the students can work on as a team challenge. If they can focus on a task rather than the "act" of connecting, the community building will naturally start to evolve.

Don't announce that "we will now build community." I love setting goals, and we set many throughout the year, but this goal is better left unstated. It's like telling people that you are trying to become their friend; the hyper-focus tends to make things weird and uncomfortable. Instead, tell the students you are happy to be their teacher and then do something together that you know actually builds community.

Don't have a million things planned. Sometimes the best beginnings of a community come from just spending low-key time together. When you plan too much or have too much to do, there isn't time for just getting to know each other, so be choosy what you invest your time in.

What Should You Do the First Week of School?

So, if you're not doing those things, what should you do? Here's my advice on fostering a creative and engaged classroom community:

Be yourself. Students can see through any phoniness, and an act is hard to keep up for more than a few days. So if you happen to have the personality of a comedian, or a perfectionist, or a massive dork (like I do), let it shine through.

Share your life. I often start my year with a video or two of my children or a funny story about one of them. Nothing planned or long, just a quick story. The students get to know me and my family, and they share their own stories as well. To see an example video that I have shown, go to http://bit.ly/1F4qLsj.

Laugh a lot. I love to laugh, and I think kids are hilarious. Give them a chance to speak in humorous ways, give them a chance to relax, and give them a chance to get to know that having a good time in allowed.

Start reworking the classroom. I stress over and over that this is "*our* classroom," so the students get to make their mark rather quickly on the classroom by moving furniture and making it usable for their needs. Believe it or not, they will begin to shape the particular learning environment that suits the particular needs of this unique group of kids.

Start learning. I know I said to go easy on curriculum the first week, but do get started with something right away. Make it fun, make it short, make it meaningful; plant a seed for what's to come and have the students see the purpose of your time together. I ask the students to tell me all about their lives as readers; see the appendix for an example survey.

Decide on expectations together. Spend some time having the students discuss what they expect out of the year and then have them discuss what that means for their learning environment. Students know how to do school (unless they are in kindergarten). Acknowledge the expertise they bring as veteran "school" children. Don't worry; the discussion can be approached again later in the year, and the expectations will probably change. Which is a wonderful thing.

Give it time. Great community does not spring up on the first day of school, but you do need to plant the first seeds that day. So tend to it and nurture it, and give it the time it deserves to grow tall and strong.

If you are looking for actual ideas of what to do with your students those first few days, see if any of these may work for you.

> Great community does not spring up on the first day of school, but you do need to plant the first seeds that day. So tend to it and nurture it, and give it the time it deserves to grow tall and strong.

- ◆ **Create flag pennants for lockers or team areas.** These easy art projects allow students to claim their locker space with pennants that have their names and whatever else they want. I cut up big sheets of 12 by 18 construction paper and give the students as many markers as I can find, they then show the world who they are through their words and art. This is a great mini-project to do as I start our first read-aloud.
- ◆ **A Wordle about me.** I have parents hand in five secret adjectives about their child, and then the students each do five of their own. We then use wordle.net to create a great piece of information to add to our classroom walls. I have also used this as a project for later in the year when I wanted students to have a nice boost in

self-confidence. Asking parents to describe their child is a great way to foster a positive relationship between school and home. If parents or guardians are unable to provide words, I have either come up with my own or asked their friends to help me out. Either way, all students get a project.

◆ **Intro to blogging.** We start to talk about blogging on the second day of school because it is a huge part of our classroom. And after we introduce blogging, we start to discuss safety. (For more on student blogging, see the related posts on my blog at http://pernillesripp. com/major-topics/student-blogging).

◆ **Name sticks, lunch magnets, and pencil cup designs.** Again, great doodling projects for the students to do as we just hang out and get to know each other. These are more suited for elementary students, so instead at the middle school level I liked having students decorate simple bookmarks for their very first book.

◆ **Writing samples.** Teachers love to see how students grow. Sampling at the very beginning of school gives me a baseline. This year we journaled on "What color is our grade?" Students write down the time it took them to write it, and I love to see whether they come at these questions from an abstract or concrete angle.

◆ **Read "Dear Future [Mrs. Ripp] Students" letters.** Every year, near the end of school, my students write a personal letter to my next-year students sharing information about our classroom and how to make it an amazing year. The new students will recall the advice all year long!

◆ **Time capsule.** When I taught fifth grade, I always had the students do a paper time capsule where they wrote down their favorite things as well as their height. Students get such a kick out of seeing how their interests have changed and how much they have grown by year's end, when we open the capsule and read them the last day of school. While I have not done this with middle school students, I could see adapting something similar with them to build community.

◆ **Make a classroom vision video.** There are many tech options here. In our room, the students come up with sentences describing their hopes and dreams for the year, and we use Animoto to make a great video (check out our vision video for 2013–14 at https://www.youtube. com/watch?v=4k3wZp2cTCU). It really starts kids thinking about their classroom environment and taking ownership of their learning.

◆ **Designing our routines.** We discuss the students' expectations of what they want their day or class to feel like. How will we get the best possible start to the year? What do we need to discuss right now?

- **The Secret Life of [Mrs. Ripp].** If you're like me, some of your students already know you, but most don't. I create a 10-picture slideshow with images/photos about myself and ask the students to guess the meaning of the pictures. Much hilarity ensues.
- **Connect the students.** This is a great activity that only requires one very large piece of paper and markers. The students all write their name on the border of the paper and then sit behind their name. The first person will make an "I like . . ." or "I do . . ." statement, and then whichever other students agree with that student all draw a line to that student's name. So if a student says, "I like soccer" then any other students that also like soccer get to connect their name to the speaker. In the end, you have a massive spider web of names connected and one very satisfied group of kids who cannot believe how much they have in common.
- **A Q&A session.** I always forget just how many questions students don't ask those very first days, so the last few years I have included a very simple Q&A session where students can either ask questions outright or write them down on a piece of paper for me to answer. In middle school, I have found this to be particularly effective since many of my students do not feel comfortable asking questions out loud but still have a lot of questions they need answered.
- **We ogle the books.** I have a rather large classroom library, one I proudly moved from elementary school to middle school, even though I wasn't sure how my seventh graders would react to it. Boy, am I glad I did. The titles are all neatly organized into bins and special care has been taken to display some of the newest and best books on that first day of school. I love seeing the students' reaction when they first meet our classroom library! While I don't allow them to grab books on the first day of school—they have to set the rules for the library first—they are allowed to browse, create wish lists, and dream of their future reading. I did this in elementary and I do it now; I am okay with being known as the teacher who is crazy about books and I want my students to know that.

No matter, what you choose to do those very first days of school, make it authentic. Make it purposeful, make it fun. The standards will still be there, as will all of the curriculum. Do not rush into the year because you are worried about not getting through everything, instead, take some time to get to know your students, let them get to know you. The investment you make in community and student relationship will always pay off later.

6

Where I Give the Classroom
Back to My Students

"Everyone's opinion matters. Everyone's voice should be heard. Students should speak up more and say what they think." —Emily A.

I didn't set out to take the classroom away from my students. I don't think any teacher does. No professor tells us that by teaching the traditional way, we will make students feel powerless and insignificant. No teacher education class provides a step-by-step plan that will make sure students know they are not the most important people in the room.

So how do I know traditional schooling often makes children feel powerless and without a voice? My students told me so. They told me through their lack of interest, their less than enthusiastic responses to questions, their yawns, their sighs. Even their eye rolls. They told me through assignments delivered in parents' handwriting, through slap-dash book reports and frustrated whispers whenever I revealed a new assignment.

Our students express their servitude when they walk silently in the hallway, dragging their feet; when recess or lunch once again tops the list of their most favorite times at school; when they glance anxiously at the clock. They tell us all the time, but do we listen?

Then: The Teacher Is the Absolute Authority

"I think students should have a voice in their education because then they won't have something at the top of their of their mind knowing that if they share it, it won't change anything."

—Tanner S.

When I was ready to give "my" classroom back to the students—to have them feel like they truly mattered—I found at least two barriers standing in the way. The first was mistrust. How could they trust me when I said this was our room, not my room? How could they believe me when I asked what and how they wanted to learn? Could I blame them if they thought this might be just another evil teacher trick (like pop quizzes and "All of the above" multiple choice answers)?

We don't teach our students to not trust us, yet many of the traditional teaching methods breed distrust. When students are asked to give their honest opinion, and a teacher then holds it against them, that teaches them a lesson. How about when we ask students to do their best but then tell them that their best is not good enough through a grade? Or tell them that there is no such thing as a dumb question but then barely withhold our laughter when a child asks a silly question? Often, some of our more innocent educational statements, intended to empower and motivate students, can have the exact opposite effect if we don't honor what we say.

And then there was the second barrier. My own demon. Control.

Control is a huge word in education. We prefer synonyms like "manage" or "supervise" or even "facilitate" but most often we're talking about control. In college, we are taught the tricks by seasoned pros, who call them "classroom management strategies." But it's not just about the classroom. We also control the learning.

The federal government decides the direction, our state decides the criteria, our district decides the curriculum, and teachers decide the how-to. If you walk by most traditional classrooms (or recall your own experience in school), the teacher is in front, desks facing forward, with quiet students raising their hands or working at their desks. The structure makes it clear who is in control in the room.

So it was in my room. I had pods, not desks, but that didn't mean I wanted the students to collaborate. I just had more room if the tables were arranged that way. I planned out every lesson as I was taught—step by step, always with a beginning, middle, and definitely an end. The goal was a finished product to be graded and handed back. One that all students would be working through at the same time, no matter their capability. End of story. Next lesson. A year consisted of a predictable number of product cycles, with students as mere producers, or at the worst of times, just bystanders. There was no shared control.

The idea of releasing control in our classrooms can be petrifying. We assume (at least I did) that the opposite of control must be chaos. If there is no clear power structure or hierarchy, no one will know how to act, behave, or learn. The students will become Wild Things, barely contained within the walls. Yet, remarkably, when I gave up total control and created a student-centered environment, chaos did not reign supreme—curiosity did, and so did experimentation.

At first, I was beyond nervous. I had nightmares imagining how much noise, clutter, and lack of learning would ensue as freedom-crazed elementary students ran amok. I should have had more faith in my students. Far from staging *Lord of the Flies*, they collaborated and supported each other. Our room seemed to sigh with satisfaction and begin to relax.

Cautiously, students opened up and shared their thoughts. They would come with lesson ideas or products they would like to try, first in protective groups and then even by themselves, spurred on by my approval. More crazy, brilliant ideas emerged than I would ever have dreamed. We were becoming "student-centered," and we did not even know that term existed.

Now: Well, You Stumped Me! How Will We Find Out?

"I think choice is one thing teachers should all do because in here we have opinions and get to discuss what we think we are doing and then we can say if what we are doing is helpful or not."

—Jordana B.

So how did the change come about?

Many experts write about how to create the perfect student-centered learning environment. I am not an expert, and I did not follow a prescribed system as I changed my teaching direction, but I did trust that little voice that had been nagging me for so long. Perhaps you have a voice as well: stop and listen to it, keep it in mind as you discover what my thinking was and start to create your own path toward giving your classroom back to students.

To me, being student-centered means putting the focus on what the students are doing rather than what the teacher is doing. I think most teachers might say they do this already, but I believe we often put on a show where the students get to watch us unfold the learning and then do some work to show they have listened. Every step of the journey through the lesson has been predetermined and planned. We've chosen the path to be traveled, and we hurry our students along so that we can get to the next thing.

In the traditional classroom, we rarely take the time to explore and meander; after all, the dictated curriculum tells us we must move on. And what if students should ask about something we haven't planned for. Or, heaven forbid, that we don't know?

So when we decide to let our students have a say about the paths we'll follow to reach our learning destinations, we have to change how we plan our days. Rather than hammering out a strict itinerary, we can work backwards, first asking ourselves what they should know when they're done exploring. In this adventurous approach to learning (they are explorers, after all), the "how" becomes just as important as the "what." And we can become explorers too.

> Rather than hammering out a strict itinerary, we can work backwards, first asking ourselves what they should know when they're done exploring. In this adventurous approach to learning (they are explorers, after all), the "how" becomes just as important as the "what."

In the truest sense of the word, what we are doing is elementary. We need to think back to kindergarten, where we taught students how to explore what they wondered about, how to share and to listen to others. We need to apply those learning strategies within our own classroom. We must discard some of the things we were diligently taught in college, draw on our own teaching and learning experiences, and let our students become investigators. Most of all, we need to stop hogging the limelight and join in the investigation.

Luckily, this process of going from a teacher-centered to a student-centered classroom is much easier than it sounds.

Next: What You Can Do, Starting Today

"Students should have a voice in their education because it makes learning feel better and less forced."

—Nathan G.

The first step toward student-driven learning is to realize that you are no longer the sole authority on learning. Again, we must reflect on our role as teachers and how we assert our control in the classroom. If you are unsure about how you do that, ask your students. Start a conversation or hand them a survey asking them to reflect on who controls the learning in the room. Do they have any say in what they are learning or how they are learning some-thing? Would they even want to have a say? (This question is great for figur-ing out how engaged students are and how we need to scaffold the change for students.) Also, ask them what the role of the teacher should be—their answers are bound to push your thinking.

Self-reflection is also key in order to change how control is handled in the classroom. You have to realize what you can let go of, and what you simply cannot. Make a list. I knew there were certain things hardwired into me that I did not want to lose control over: good manners, for example, and high expectations for their work. Yet many other things—like sitting at desks, rubrics, grading, and homework—I could let go of gladly.

Baby steps are always best because students, just like us, are used to a cer-tain way of doing school. They are also used to certain kinds of teachers, and as I've said here, they're going to be naturally mistrustful when a teacher says "Hey, we're going to be partners." Trust will come, but it has to grow natu-rally too. So start these deeper conversations with students and then mind your reaction. It is vital that students see your reaction as a positive one and not one of judgment.

It's also likely that students coming from other grades and classrooms will not be at all prepared for student-centered learning. Some, instead, will insist on knowing how to get that "A." We have to help them rediscover the true learner's voice that they've always been asked to leave outside the classroom door.

And we can start doing that during the first week of school.

Here Are Some First Steps:

◆ Use some of the ideas at the end of Chapter 5 to begin building trust and community. One of the first things I do is have my new students create the classroom rules (really create them) and also help design and set up the classroom. Through these two simple, but powerful, exercises students start to take ownership of our learning environment, thinking about how they learn best, and learning to trust the teacher and each other.

◆ Make sure you speak to your students about *why* you want to change the way they are accustomed to doing school. This is a great conversation to have as early as possible in the year. In language that will make sense to them, share the rationale behind your decision. Explain why you think students learn better this way and ask for their opinion.

◆ If this is a change with a group of students you have been teaching for a while, take time to discuss how the journey you are embarking on will be a challenging one and perhaps unlike any other they've experienced. For me, it was incredible to see the students get excited about all of my crazy ideas. Our first conversation turned into a great discussion session where they were already starting to test the waters, seeing how serious I was and how much of their own thinking they could share with me.

◆ If you are radically changing your classroom, you have to get parents on board; after all, these are their children we get to teach. Many parents are open to new ideas as long as they understand the *why* behind them. Do not be afraid to share with them. (More about parents in the next chapters.) And you may also find resistance from colleagues. What I have found to be true is that people fear the unknown, so be an open book about why you are changing the way you are teaching, and don't expect others to change because you did. Too often we are sledgehammers with our new ideas, forcing them upon others, where instead we need to just share about our journey and perhaps plant a seed of inspiration that way.

Once you have set the stage for this different learning journey, it is time to do some actual learning. This is where you have to walk the walk.

What Student-Centered Learning Looks Like

"Students should have a choice because different kids have different interest. We should have a baseline of what you have to learn but if we really take into consideration what the class wants, you will definitely have better effort, and grades may go up because of it."

—Meghan D.

There are many books out there on the topic of student-centered learning, and I must confess I did not follow the path of any of them. Instead, I chose to find my own way, inspired by conversations and blog posts I had read. I encourage you to do the same—explore, read, experiment. Don't rely on a single authority, including me. In the end, this book is really aimed at encouraging you to discover what works for you. What I'll do here is reflect some on my own journey in the hope that my story will suggest some directions to explore.

When some people hear that I do "student-centered learning," they envision a classroom free from standards. Yet the reality is I have standards to meet, essential learner outcomes to follow, curriculum to cover, and yes, those darling standardized tests. So no, my room isn't some test-free haven, but a totally typical public school classroom with many students who are all on vastly different levels. They all have different talents and challenges, and just want to succeed and have some fun in school.

And yet, amidst all of the demands and expectations from higher up, student-centered learning still worked for me, whether it was in the upper elementary classroom or in the middle school one. And it can work for you too.

It's best to start small. At the elementary level, I did this by choosing one subject that lends itself particularly well to student-centered learning: social studies. While I had some sense of how I wanted the students to experience the rest of our curriculum, I had to try out some ideas before I really let go.

Social studies, and science for that matter, lend themselves to exploration because students have usually done more investigative learning within these topics before they enter your class. It doesn't take as much convincing to get them to explore and possibly experience some failure in these subjects. The stakes probably don't seem as high as they are in literacy or math, where much of the high-stakes testing is focused.

Of course you can begin with any topic or subject you choose. Start experimenting in the area where you feel most comfortable. By diving into a single topic, we got our feet wet, figured out how to swim through it, and then we started to look for other pools to explore. If you begin with a project you feel fairly certain you can manage, you will avoid panic. And that is very important, because panic is contagious.

When I moved to the middle school in Oregon, Wisconsin, I was delighted to take the position as a seventh grade English teacher, yet had no idea of how to create personalized learning within the English curriculum. After all, as an elementary teacher where I taught many subjects, the pressure was not nearly as great to have a passionate literacy environment because we would get more hands-on, choice-based exploration within science and social studies. With those two subjects no longer being at my disposal, the challenge to create a passionate learning environment seemed daunting, even for me. Yet the past many months have proven to me that you can indeed give the classroom back to your students and follow these ideas at most ages, with any subject. (I say "most" because I have no experience with kindergarten and will therefore not pretend that it will work in the same way as it did with fourth graders.)

Your First Student-Centered Lesson

1. **Know your goals.** You cannot set students on a journey if you have no idea what the destination is. I have said this before, but it is so important. Your goal can be the creation of or mastery of something;

it does not have to always be an actual product that is created, nor does it have to be of a certain size. Some ideas or concepts require more in-depth learning because the goal encompasses more things. Others may be quick mini-lessons meant to secure only one skill. Just be clear about where you are going, and how that destination—close by or far away—relates to the big curriculum picture. PBL, or Project Based Learning, has been on the rise in education in the past few years. While many of my ideas support the PBL philosophy, I am not necessarily advocating for it at all times. I would rather advocate for a nuanced approach where students' goals change with need and expand with their growth. Sometimes we do not need a full project to master a skill but rather a conversation, so please do not feel pressured to always make it hands-on.

2. **Then rewrite and break down your goal so it makes sense to students and to yourself.** I do this in my head; others will want to put it into words on screen or paper. Some of our essential learner outcomes are so lofty that I can only use them as a guide. How is that lofty goal going to actually look in real life? For example: "Using the writing process" (lofty goal) might require a breakdown into five different goals, each with different outcomes. With today's focus on the Common Core and similar expectations, understanding and interpreting the standards is vital as you work through your curriculum. So take the time to put the goal of your first student-driven learning activity into your own words.

Once you have done your thinking, it is necessary that your students do theirs. Standards or criteria for learning should not be an afterthought, nor should it be in an inaccessible language to students. If we truly want students to master certain learning, then they have to take full ownership of it; the first step toward that is deconstructing the standards and rewriting them in student language, which, of course, the students should be a part of.

3. **Brainstorm some ideas before you introduce.** I love coming up with ideas about what types of projects we can do to reach our goals, and then telling my students about them as a way to start the discussion, particularly at the beginning of the year. That way, if this expansion of student choice is new to them, they don't feel overwhelmed. Some kids will be totally energized when we ask "How are you going to reach the goal?" Others will look like they are about to cry. Give those

uncertain kids some scaffolding and point them in the right direction; they will learn to take on more and more responsibility as they get used to this approach. I promise.

4. **Give the introduction enough time.** When you reveal the first big adventure, you do not want to be in a hurry. You want to get the kids excited, but you also want them to understand the purpose and the direction of what you are about to undertake. If you hurry you will regret it later—which leads to the next tip.

5. **Let the kids do it.** Let the kids think of questions. Let them pick partners, even if you are thinking you would never pair "those two." (You will sometimes be very surprised!) Let the kids try out a direction and let them struggle a little bit. You can always jump in—but don't do it right away. Resist as long as you can. You can gently redirect or even advise, but don't take over. So often we teachers take over much too soon. For this to work you have to trust your students.

6. **Step aside.** For this work to be truly student-centered, the sage has to get off of the stage. Take off your teacher hat and put on your facilitator hat. Remember these kids are here to experience school, not just to have it done to them. Put them on the stage. I know we think we need to scaffold at the first sign of student anxiety (and with some kids, you *may* need to), but the large majority of students will work through it if you give them the room, time, and trust to explore their projects.

7. **Give them time to discuss.** The best ideas often come from students. Give them the time to figure things out. I know I don't write the best lessons when I am rushed, when I don't have time to ponder, so create that thinking time for your students. Have them discuss with others, let them mull over it. They don't have to come up with a firm direction right away. Sometimes projects occur naturally because their curiosity takes over, and that is something to celebrate indeed. Be ready to jump in with some ideas to get them thinking, while continuing to let them lead the conversation. It can take time to find the right balance between your ideas and theirs, so do not beat yourself up if it doesn't work out right away. As we know, all students need different things at different times; they will get to a point where this process becomes natural for them.

8. **Don't fret about the volume.** One thing I learned was that student-centered learning can get really noisy at times. And that's okay. Most of the time, the noise gets louder because students are discussing their ideas with each other (or speaking to you about them) and they are just really excited. I would rather have my classroom loud with excitement then silent with boredom. And the same goes for physical activity—abandon the "stay in your seat" thing too. Let them move around as they like, get comfortable, and get working. Do find a balance between loud excitement and quiet contemplation. Learning looks different for different tasks and there should be room for it all.

9. **Expect failure.** And then learn from it. Not all projects are going to be stellar, not all work will be immaculate, and that is okay, too. These kids are learning, and the missteps can lead to a wonderful discussion about what went wrong and where do we go from there. Isn't that what scientists, authors, and engineers do? Behind the noise and activity is a powerful learning process, and there simply is no such thing as failure (unless they do not show up). They may not have learned as much as you were hoping for, it's true. So what's next?

10. **Make room for it all.** Not all learning will be project based. Sometimes there will be no end product but rather a discussion, an idea to play with, or a new direction taken. This isn't the "teach the material—give the test" kind of schooling. Instead it's "get to know the material, get invested, and show me you are gaining skills, knowledge, and understanding." I've had kids who wanted to take a test, and that was fine with me. I've had kids who wanted to make a movie to show their learning, and I said, great! And I've had kids who just want to tell me all about it. Wahoo! Make room for all types of assessment, give a deadline, check on their progress, and hold them accountable. Student-centered does not always mean "project." It means giving them a voice and a choice. In the middle school setting, where you teach a hundred or more students, I have found it better to approach students, offering them a chance to show mastery, rather than wait for them to approach me. I tell them a set deadline for when mastery should be achieved and then continuously monitor, check in, and support as needed. A few weeks before the deadline, I start to ask students whether they are ready to hand something in, have a conversation, or prove their mastery

in whichever way they have developed. Sometimes I schedule appointments with them so that students know specifically when they will be held accountable, but it depends on the group and the concept we are working with.

Lessons Learned Along the Way

I started out on this student-centered journey knowing that I had to offer my students more time for true collaboration, not just teacher-directed "cooperation." I knew as well that I had to give them control in the classroom. I started out dreaming, not quite sure what it would look like, what the products would be, or even if the learning would be enhanced (or actually suffer).

Five years into this type of learning, I'm not so dreamy-eyed. I have experienced some affirmations and some humbling realizations:

◆ **Not all units lend themselves well to choice, but it is doable.** It can be a challenge to cover the material you feel you need to cover—in a textbook for example—while staying student-centered. I have spent many nights thinking up how I could possibly engage my students in something without just lecturing. It takes time, but it's time well spent when you see the students light up at what they will be doing.

◆ **It also gets easier.** After a while your brain switches from "How will I present this?" to "How will the students work with this?" There's a subtle but important shift here, and as you work through it, you create a toolbox of ways to get students to take charge of learning. And if you include students in the planning process, you have many more ideas, so that leads me to:

◆ **Include the students!** When I am stumped over how to make a unit more engaging, I bring the puzzle to those most affected: the kids. It does not have to be a long conversation; once they are used to being asked, a quick brainstorm will do. It is amazing to see what they come up with.

◆ **Trust the students.** There have been self-selected student teams that I have shuddered at inwardly, and in the end they created beautiful projects. There have also been times where we needed to have some serious reflection about whether a particular combination was effective. That's okay, so long as you include the students involved in the conversation and don't just make the decision that a partnership doesn't work. Sometimes we are too quick to decide what collaboration should look like; sometimes a discussion can improve a team's effectiveness.

◆ **Be honest with the students.** I have very high expectations for projects, and I have called students out on poor work quality. There is a way to do this, though, without creating a "Battle Hymn of the Tiger Mother" scenario. Ask them to evaluate their own work, even midway through a project, and take time to reflect. Point out what you see as a possible gap and help them out. Not all students can create wonderful things at the drop of a hat.

◆ **Scaffolding at various levels.** Some students just need an idea and they fly, others need hand holding and even a cheer or two before they get off the ground, and some are just too boxed in to even know where to start. Get to know your students and their work styles, and tailor your scaffolding accordingly. Invest the time in relationship building and you will see direct results in their output.

◆ **It will not always work.** I have had some epic ideas that turned out absolutely terrible. Or we have let ideas get so complicated that the students lose interest. There have been times when the environment was just wrong and the work wasn't fun. Or when a project has taken too long and the interest level has faded to near zero. It's going to happen. And yet I don't give up. I keep going because I see how invested the students are over the days and weeks and months of the year. I see how excited they get to use their hands and their minds, to explore on their own with guidance from me, to learn from each other.

My dream—more and more realized every day—is to have a classroom where students make choices and always have a voice. I see how invested they are now in their own education. I know that is something lecturing will never, ever do for them. Education no longer is something done to them; it's something they own and manipulate. School is not just a place where they absorb information from adults. They learn to take information, examine its quality, and use the best of it to create and innovate. Yet, convincing people that students should be given shared control of the classroom can sometimes feel like a suicide mission. Say "personalized learning" and some people may think you have lost your mind or are looking for way to not teach much any more. Even now, when personalized learning or student choice and voice has become more of a respected approach to teaching, I still meet resistance wherever I go. In fact, some educators or districts are quite against it, but for many different reasons. I cannot be alone in seeing this resistance, so I thought a discussion of what those barriers may be and how you can approach a discussion to work around them, would be in order.

Barrier: It's one more thing to do. We are faced with seemingly more tasks every single year as teachers, from major ones forced upon us to the little ones we cannot wait to do because we were inspired. When will we ever find the time to do this type of teaching as well?

Discussion point: This should not be an add-on but a replacement. So if you are already doing something, change it with a lens of giving students more control. Can you add choice into a preexisting project? Can students show mastery in a multitude of ways? Embrace personalized learning as a way to become a better educator by sharing more control with the students. Keep it manageable for you and integrate in a natural way to alleviate the feeling of one more thing being added to the to-do list.

Barrier: It is overwhelming. It is easy to see why giving the classroom back to your students can be viewed as overwhelming. Often those who discuss its merits have been doing it for years and have framed their whole classroom around it. Their teaching and learning initiatives are a long list of to-do's.

Discussion point: One small step at a time. When discussing this type of philosophical change, focus on how to start, what to do in the beginning, and the small changes that can make a big difference. Certainly keep the end-point in mind, but don't worry about it yet. Worry about where you are right now and how you will start your journey, not when you are going to get to the end.

Barrier: It will be chaotic. We often envision chaos when we stop doing a one-path-to-the-learning format for students and that when students are given choice they will not know what to do.

Discussion point: Giving the classroom back to students does not mean giving up control, but rather that control is shared with the students. It also means multiple paths to mastery, but these are planned out either by yourself or in conjunction with your students. Yet, you know yourself best, what you can give up control of and what you can not. You are also a member of this learning community, so if there are certain things that need to stay in order—such as an assignment being done a certain way, or students sitting in a particular way—it is okay to hold onto that. Find the things that you can let go of, invite student input into the process, and grow together.

Barrier: My subject matter won't work. This type of teaching means hands-on and project based. How do you do that in English, Spanish, or any other class?

Discussion point: Student voice and choice can be implemented into any classroom, the lens just has to switch. I had a lot easier time giving choice in social studies and science because a lot of our learning was hands-on, project based. So when I switched to just teaching English, I had to change my way of thinking. This means students have choice in how they show mastery (different project choices), when they show mastery (timeline), and often how they work within the classroom (classroom setup/management).

Barrier: It will be replaced with another idea soon. Education is a long list of new ideas and change is the one constant we have.

Discussion point: Changing the way you teach and offering students shared control really just means great teaching, and great teaching will not be replaced with a new idea. So while new initiatives are bound to come, the ideas helping you be a better teacher remain because they speak to student autonomy and reigniting a passion for learning.

Barrier: I don't want to integrate more technology, or don't have access. Technology inequity is a real problem. So is technology fear. Some teachers want to feel comfortable with the technology they bring in before students use it, and others will never be able to get the things they wish they could.

Discussion point: Creating a passionate learning environment is not about the technology. It is about creating an education process that takes into account the needs and desires of each child, while still working through the set curriculum. Technology is a tool that can be used in this process but not a central tenet. I started out with four computers in my room for 26 students. We naturally did not incorporate a lot of technology, and we didn't need to. Choices involved the things we did have and students bringing in things from home if they wanted to. We made it work with what we had.

Barrier: I won't be a good teacher. It is hard to change the way we teach because we may already be teaching really well.

Discussion point: Change is hard for all of us, but modeling risks for students is instrumental in their learning journey. I am uncomfortable every time I make a big decision about the way

I teach or something we will do, but I think the discomfort makes me a more thoughtful practitioner. By sharing and modeling this for students, I am showing them that I take risks and that sometimes those risks pay off and other times they don't. We have to grow to evolve and sometimes that means even leaving behind things that were just fine. Besides, our students change every year, so should we.

Barrier: I have to do the same as all the other teachers in my subject or grade level. We don't want students to be a part of an educational lottery where the quality of their education hinges on which teacher they get, so sometimes uniformity and in turn, conformity, is preached above all else.

Discussion point: Have what other teachers do as one of the choices for students. This brilliant idea was shared at the task force meeting I was a part of in my district in Oregon, Wisconsin. Instead of dismissing what other teachers are doing, simply make it one of the paths that students can take. That way you are also catering to the myriad of ways that students learn. You may learn best in a hands-on project-based environment, whereas others may learn best with a read/reflect/discuss with a test at the end pathway. Make room for all of your learners and include the ways of other teachers in your room.

Barrier: Parents/administrators/community will be upset. When we are faced with unknowns our first instinct may be to revolt.

Discussion point: School should look different than when we were students. Yet communication, understanding, and examples are vital when integrating more student voice and choice into your classroom our school. Any change is hard for parents who want to try to help their children, so make sure you are communicating the why and the how behind your changes, whatever they may be. If administration is wary, bring them in to see the change, show them other classrooms, and explain your motivation. Tell them you will do a trial period and you can discuss and evaluate. Just like you are asking others to be open to change, be open to frank discussion yourself.

Giving the classroom back to my students has been one of the most significant changes I ever did in my educational journey, but it wasn't always smooth. I have faced many of these barriers myself but now love being in a district that has it as part of its vision. Wherever you are in your journey, or even if you haven't started, don't be discouraged by the barriers that may face you. Reach out, connect with others who are on the same journey, and find the support you need to be successful. I am here to help if you need it.

Voice Is Only Meaningful If Someone Is Listening

When you give students a voice, it comes with a caveat. You must listen to that voice and not be offended.

When you give students a voice, it comes with a caveat. You must listen to that voice and not be offended. That does not mean that students get a carte blanche to tear apart your classroom without any point to their criticism, but it does mean that you have to grow some thicker skin. It is not easy being told that something you are doing is boring, or that a child still hates school, but in the end I would rather have a child feel comfortable enough to express those feelings than for a child to tell me whatever they think I want to hear.

I encourage you to set up opportunities for students to share their opinions with you. I also encourage you to model how to share opinions in a kind and civil manner, as this is a life skill that all students will need. There is a right way to offer up suggestions and it is vital that we practice this with students. Pick a format for the conversations and then give the students time to have them.

I use blogging as a way to take the pulse of my classroom on a regular basis, but we also have classroom meetings, surveys, and small conversations that allow students to express their opinion. As teachers we are quick to ask for feedback from our administration or even colleagues, but how often do we ask it from our students? Make their feedback a natural part of your classroom and use it to change what you can and create a better environment.

As you shift toward a more student-driven learning environment, don't ever stop questioning yourself. I certainly do not have all of the answers. There will be times when you are firmly in your teacher role, but if you are true to your commitment, your classroom will become more and more about them and less and less about you, because your students will demand it. As teachers we cannot be the only people in the room whose ideas and voices matter.

Student Voice: Let Me Count the Ways

Giving students a voice is something I discuss often with others. It may even be what lead you to this book. The questions I get most often are: How do I know that I am doing that? What does it look like? While I've discussed some of this already, an action list can come in handy as you prepare yourself to make the big change.

Curriculum: Give them ownership. Even within the strictest dictated curriculum, we can still share ownership with our students, by giving them the right to create something they choose. If the format is predetermined, then give them a choice over the topic. If the topic is predetermined, then give them choice in the format. Presentation, collaboration, and assessment are also areas where you can give students a voice. You just have to find the time to ask them. Ask yourself: Do my students have a say in what they are doing right now?

Classroom routine: I don't make the rules of our classroom; my students and I do. We discuss them at the beginning of the year and then we modify them as we go. They have a voice and a right to decide how their classroom will run. We have nonnegotiables such as respecting others and then go from there. Every year is different because every group is different. Ask yourself: Who set the rules of the classroom?

Classroom setup: Students can't have a voice if we dictate the way the classroom space is organized. We can enforce our agenda just as easily through our setup as through our words. Where is the teacher's desk located? How is it faced? Where is the main area of the room? Where is the focal point? Can students shape and manipulate the physical classroom? Can they move desks, tables, areas? Do they decide where they work? Do they decide how they work? All of this gives them a voice. Ask yourself: Where do my students work? What is the vibe of the room?

Assessment: I do not believe in the power of a report card or in the power of grades, so students and I discuss what a well-done product should look like. Our assessments grow out of those discussions. My students *self-reflect* a lot and set goals. They discuss goals with me, with their parents, and with each other. We strive for accountability and also a deeper understanding of what it means to create. Ask yourself: Who determines the grade? Who establishes the guidelines?

Outlets for voice: Students must know that they have somewhere they can always turn to speak to each other, to me, to the world. Our *student blogs* do that for us, and I encourage them to speak freely. Many of them do and I always grow from what they post. So find an outlet for their voice (blogs, Twitter, videos, posters and pin-its . . . there are lots of possibilities) so that they know someone is listening. Ask yourself: Where do I hear my students' voices? Where does the world hear them?

Face to face: When my students speak, I listen. I stop whatever I am doing and I look at them. I listen, I respond, and things sometimes are fixed or changed. We meet as a group every Friday to discuss achievements, share advice, or just check in. We speak in the morning before the day really gets going so that students know what to expect, know what their day looks like, and what our expectations are. I am accountable to them. Even if they have complaints, they know I will take them to heart, without negative repercussions. I never hold a grudge and my actions show that. Ask yourself: What do I do when students speak to me? How do I react?

Simple Ideas for Big Change

Change the way they sit. I ask my students to sit wherever they want as long as they can work. Only once in awhile do I have to interfere as to their seating choice. I have much happier students. Why? Because they got to have a say in their classroom environment, they were given control.

Change the way they work. I ask my students to discover how they work best. Do they like to hand-write things, type, dictate? Are they kids who love to write papers rather than make a movie? How do they want to read? How do they want to think? If students are to discover how they work best, we have to give them choice and room for exploration. This doesn't mean that every single thing has to be open for anything, but simply providing choice in some things is a step in the right direction.

Change the knowledge they have. One pushback against personalized learning has been that students don't necessarily know what they need to know, and I agree. That is why personalized learning also has to include exposing students to various topics, such as the materials we have to cover due to standards. However, there are many ways to expose students to these topics, so don't do the same thing over and over; change it up and allow for student ideas in the way material is covered.

Change the expectations for all. We tend to teach the way we learn best but that is not always the way our students learn best. So rather than plan by yourself, plan with your students. Their ideas are often much better than ours anyway. This also allows us to move out of our comfort zone rather than use the same type of format, or go with just your own thinking. So ask the students *how* they would like to learn something and then heed their advice. You don't have to go with every single idea but try a few of them at least.

Change the timeline. I used to think all students had to gain mastery of something at the same time because I had taught it to them all at the same time, until I had my twins. Kids, even born at roughly the same time from the same mother, do not learn things at the same time. Why do we expect our students to? My students will now show me mastery of the standards when they feel they are ready within the quarter. Sure, it will require a more lucid timeline, but it really doesn't add more work for me—all I need is a more flexible mindset.

Change the conversation. I used to be the queen of all answers and solutions. If a student had a problem, I fixed it. If a student needed help, I helped them. I used to think that was one of my main components of being a teacher: the helper/fixer/teacher role. Now I know that students need support so they can help themselves and figure things out themselves, and my language reflects that. Rather than giving an answer, I ask a question back. Rather than affirming an answer, I ask them to explain it. I ask for their input; I ask them to reflect; I ask them to provide solutions and to teach others what they know. This classroom is no longer about what I need them to do or know, but what they need to do or know, and that carries power. So change the way you speak, include the students in the conversation, and stick with it.

Letting Go of the Punish, Behave, Reward Cycle

"How do you know who the bad students are? They act different than the normal students." —Jonah P.

"Put your name on the board!" Those words spoken in a very stern voice accompanied by a teacher look was enough to whip the toughest student into shape in my room. Except when it didn't, which for me was enough times to make me wonder: could my discipline systems really be discarded and replaced with . . . nothing?

Then: The Teacher as Lawgiver

"Should teachers reward students? No, students need to just pay attention and not want candy."

—Preston R.

If you had come by my room those first few years you would have seen the sticks in cups or names on the board with checks (sometimes double checks)—and plenty of stern teacher looks to go around. I was doing exactly what I had been taught in college, exerting my control as the main authority figure, and if students misbehaved, then there was going to be some form of punishment.

Oh, there were plenty of rewards as well. If students didn't move their stick or get their name on the board for a week, then they were entered into a drawing for a pizza lunch with me. At the end of the month, if they didn't have their name in my book for failing to turn in their homework, they could also enter the drawing. When I finally drew names, five lucky students would eat some pizza with the teacher. Confused? I was! I could hardly keep track of all those names, checks, and punishments.

Gold stars, super-duper stickers, tri-colored cups, names on the board . . . I have done it all. And when one reward/punishment system failed, another one took over. Never one to sit and reflect that perhaps it was the system that was faulty and not just that the students grew tired of it, I persisted with carrots and sticks as if my very life depended on it. And so I thought: tight discipline = teaching success.

What's more, those stickers meant I cared. That Awesome Board where A work was proudly displayed gave students something to strive for. That certificate I awarded for an A on your math test meant you were smart and that other students should look up to you. Right?

Oh, I thought I was clever. I knew how to motivate, and after all, what could a little reward do that would possibly hurt the child? Then I read Alfie Kohn's book *Punished by Rewards* and realized just how wrong I had been. Those papers on the Awesome Board did nothing to create a learning community in our classroom. Instead, my bright display acted as a great divide, sorting students into two simplistic groups: "can" and "cannot." Those stickers I doled out for anything above 90% were not a cheerful way to celebrate achievement but rather a glaring marker showing which students were most willing to learn the way the teacher wanted them to.

By perpetually focusing negative energy on the same students (who were often the ones having their name singled out somehow already), I was truly just adding to their self doubt. While I believe in discipline for all students, I also believe in compassion, and that philosophy simply was not fitting in with my chosen systems.

So I did the only thing I knew how: I threw it all out again; however, this time instead of hunting for a new system, I decided to detox myself, start the year with no system for reward and punishment, and instead strive to create a classroom community where students just knew what the expectation is. I was terrified.

Now: Let's Talk About It

"In my experience, when kids misbehave they do it because they are bored. If teachers make school a place kids want to be, kids will behave."

—Rachel J.

I believed the carrot-and-stick approach was the best way to control a class-room. Now I know that control is not what you want—community is—and punishment and rewards will never build that.

Now I believe rewards twist the focus of the classroom and provide students with a false reason to want to engage. I believe that rewards always end up benefiting the same students and some are always left out. I know some will say that classroom-wide rewards are the answer to that inequity, but ask yourself: how often have you taken away classroom points or not given marbles to the group based on the actions of one kid or just a couple?

The bottom line for me is when we perpetually stick a carrot in front of students' faces—whether it be through points, letters or marbles—we are teaching them that they should not do anything without a reward. So while in the short term it may work to have kids get points to earn something as a classroom, in the long run it is not shaping their behavior around the idea that they want to behave simply for the greater good.

I need kids who want to be in my classroom and I expect kids to take responsibility for their behaviors. So I do not make kids "earn" anything in the reward sense, and I do not single out kids. Instead we celebrate class-wide whenever an occasion arises. Celebrations are given, not earned, and they can be based on whether we have achieved something or because it's a certain time of year. Often students and I discuss how we should celebrate something and the opportunity to celebrate is never ever taken away from them. I never use it as a way to manipulate their behavior or to point out anything. We simply celebrate, and there is always a lot to celebrate! I would rather teach and help create an environment where students are intrinsically motivated to be part of that community. While extrinsic motivators such as tangible rewards may work in the short term, over time they lose their effectiveness and teachers then have to up the ante or the reward. We end up in a vicious cycle where students only learn to earn something, rather than learn to become more knowledge-able people. The internal satisfaction or intrinsic reward that a student gets from handling a difficult learning task or mastering a new concept is what we should be celebrating, not diminishing it by handing them a gold star or another point toward a party. The learning should be the reward in itself.

> The bottom line for me is when we perpetually stick a carrot in front of students' faces—whether it be through points, letters or marbles—we are teaching them that they should not do anything without a reward.

In the beginning, when I gave up my inane discipline plans, I braced myself for the anarchy to come. Out went the sticks, the cups, the pointed fingers, the lost recesses. No more raised voice telling students that they better behave or else; no more threats of phone calls home. Instead, we had conversation, and lots of it. We talked together about expectations (high ones at that), and we wondered about the meaning of respect—respect for us as a learning community and respect for each student as an individual with rights, and feelings and responsibilities. Students were not minions or Wild Things to be corralled and controlled. With respect at the center of our community, we didn't need rewards—no parties or pizza or coupons for good behavior. Out it all went, just like that.

That first year, I'll admit, was nerve-wracking. I held my breath because I couldn't be sure what to expect. Today was good, but what about tomorrow? I thought for sure that eventually the students would take advantage of me, would be sneaky and subversive. But that never happened. If just one child was off during a day—disruptive, disrespectful, and so forth—it was usually handled through a quiet conversation off to the side or right at his or her table. Sometimes we went into the hallway.

work on this! → I tried to limit the times I called out their names, and I was respectful in how I spoke to them. No more teacher from the top; no more "I am going to get you if you don't listen," but instead an invitation for them to evaluate how their behavior was affecting their learning and the learning of their classmates.

I also had to make sure the learning was something they did not want to miss. If the experience was dull or repetitive, asking them to consider how their behavior was affecting their learning would bear no weight. I believe this is why we are taught to take away recess; since it is fun, and students look forward to the break, we can hit them where it hurts the most. If the learning itself becomes fun, engaging, exciting, collaborative, then asking students to step away from the learning means something. They want to participate and not miss out.

Even with this new approach, it's true that sometimes my class was just off—jumpy, jiggly, or falling asleep. In the past, I would have yelled and probably lectured about the importance of school. Of course, that approach never seemed to startle them back into learning mode. In my reconfigured classroom, I came to see that if a day arose where the students seemed off, it was up to me to modify or change the planned activities.

Sometimes I would try to include movement, extra discussion, some humor—anything just to get them tuned in. The learning goals usually stayed the same; after all, we did have a curriculum to complete. But the methodology behind the delivery would change, emphasizing whatever I felt my students needed that day to keep them engaged. Over time it became clear that poor behavior tended to arise when students were bored or disengaged. My worst days were those where I had not considered the needs of my students—those days with too much sitting and too little choice. The result was something like "instant karma," training me to become better and better at keeping the focus on what students need.

So you're still wondering: How hard was it not to have a punishment system? In the beginning, very. Instinctively, I wanted to yell out "Move your stick!" I sometimes had to grind my teeth. It got easier with time. The students would know when they were misbehaving because we would discuss it. If the whole class or a majority of students were off, we had a class meeting. Yes, we spent a lot of time talking—but really, I would have spent about the same amount of time yelling at the kids and never coming closer to a resolution.

In this way, we grew together. The students got used to it; they did not take advantage, but instead relished the fact that they had a voice in their classroom and were expected to help fix the problem—not just rely on the teacher's heavy-handedness. They knew what the behavior expectations were for the different learning scenarios because we'd discussed them the first week of school. This was our classroom, not just mine.

It worked. It still works. I would never go back to the way I once ruled over my classroom.

I did not take away recess. I did reserve recess time to work with the kids who needed extra one-on-one. I made fewer phone calls home. I sent one child twice to the office that first year (for recess related issues). I know there are tougher situations out there than mine, but this was your average American elementary classroom. I had the talkers, the interrupters, the disrespectful, the fighters and the sleepers. And inviting them to join and share responsibility for a genuine community worked for those kids as well.

My students felt part of something bigger than just my classroom, and they let me know on the last day of school just how much it meant to them. They relished the voice they had, even when it came to setting their own consequences. They loved that rewards were no longer personal but rather classroom-wide—that together we would decide when we had something to celebrate and how it should be celebrated. Students were not singled out for horrible behavior, and so I no longer had "that kid" that everyone knew would get in trouble. Instead, we were all there as learners, being rewarded through our community rather than punished.

It had not been chaos, it had worked, and my mind was made up. I threw away my sticks and cups for good that last day of school.

Next: What You Can Do, Starting Today

"I know all students like rewards, but the truth is the teachers are giving us [an] education, which we will need through our whole lives."

—Isabel O.

Abandon your punishment and rewards system. Or at least question why you need such a system and how effective it really is. Here are some questions I pondered as I made my decision:

- **Does the punishment fit the crime?** Often we punish students by taking away recess or by sending them to the office. There are a few things wrong with this. Recess is often exactly what a kid filled with energy needs, so taking it away only exacerbates the problem. Sending a child to the office in anger only solidifies the power struggle that they have sparked with you and leaves you powerless as far as outcome. While I do send students to the office, it is most often for a break, not a meeting with the principal.
- **Do the punishment/rewards always happen to the same students?** If so, then the problem is too deep for punishment to fix. As each school year begins, most teachers can tell you exactly which kid will be the one to get punished the most. Often it's a boy with too much energy or a total disconnect to school. When I moved away from a punishment mindset, that same kid whom I would have labeled a troublemaker became a mystery to solve instead. Now we work together to try to figure out how to make the year an optimal experience. The time spent yelling is now spent engaging.
- **Do student behaviors change because of the punishments/rewards?** Often we see short-term behavior changes, but I have yet to see students who were punished into permanently changing their ways. What I have experienced instead: the same kid is punished over and over (whether by removal of rights or deeper consequences), gets stuck in the role of Troublemaker, and continues the cycle of bad behavior. Most often bad behavior in the classroom reflects our failure to truly engage children or something deeper happening within them. It is our job to figure out what's going on.
- **Do other students perpetually witness particular students losing privileges?** In my classroom, this used to be the case. I would single out the kids who were misbehaving in front of everyone else so that I could make an example of them. Unfortunately, this tends to backfire. The power struggle ensues, and those kids get perpetually labeled by the rest of the students. Not many of the "good kids" want to be their friends. Think of the long-term damage that being singled out repeatedly can have on a child. I did, and I cannot do it any longer.
- **Do the punishments/rewards divide your classroom?** We had the good kids who were rewarded with pizza lunches and gold stickers,

and then we had the bad kids who missed recess and got phone calls home. The composition of the groups rarely changed once they were determined during the first weeks of school.

- **Do your students fear you or respect you?** Some of my students worked because I asked them to, others worked because they knew I would punish them if they didn't. Learning should be joyous, not fearful. If intimidation is the only reason students produce work then it is time we re-examine our own classroom management style and teaching methodologies.

- **Are your students driven by material gains and losses?** I had students who would read only because they knew they would get a prize. They got no pleasure from what they were reading; instead, they sped through books so they could get to the reward at the end. This is hardly a great reason to read, and it's a strategy that teaches students to see reading as something we only do for personal material gain. Intrinsic rewards. Love of reading. That's what we should be cultivating.

- **Does my need to punish block my understanding of what is really happening with a child?** This was a big one for me. It's easier to punish than it is to find the time to discover what's actually going on with a child. I had a student who hardly ever finished any math homework, and every time this happened I required him to finish it during recess. After several months it finally occurred to me to dig a little deeper. I got beyond his "I don't have time" reply and discovered that his mother worked a night shift. He was alone in their apartment and scared every night. Mind you, this was a 9-year old. Homework was definitely not on his list of priorities, and it really didn't need to be. We scaled back on the take-home math assignments, and he had one less thing to worry about every day as he joined his friends for recess.

- **Am I perpetuating a cycle of destructive feelings toward school when I punish a student?** Some kids hate school by the time they are in late elementary. Somehow the school and the teachers within it have destroyed every bit of love for learning and innate curiosity with too much punishment and too many rules. Once I removed punishment from the equation, I was able to form better relationships with students who were beginning to hate school. Through these relationships we discovered how much fun school can be. I want my students to leave my classroom still loving learning, not dreading the next decade of their life.

- **Is there a different way to motivate without using punishment or rewards?** Yes, yes, yes! Read on.

Learn New Ways to Motivate

Not punishing students does not mean letting things slide or letting them walk all over you. It simply means handling situations calmly, figuring out the "why" behind the behavior, and then working on that rather than enforcing a set of rules. How you react changes from situation to situation—something that's much more difficult to do when you have cut rules into stone the first week of school.

Much of misbehavior comes from students' perception of control within the classroom. That perception also affects their intrinsic motivation for wanting to be successful participants. A problem with punishment and reward is that it often only motivates in the short term. And yet many teachers do not know how else to get students to behave. I certainly was not consistently successful until I realized that the problem wasn't the students, it was more often the curriculum and how I taught it. Meaning, it was really me.

> A problem with punishment and reward is that it often only motivates in the short term. And yet many teachers do not know how else to get students to behave.

While I may not be the one who decides what to teach, I am most certainly the one who decides *how* to teach it. If I thought that mostly lecturing (which even put me to sleep in college) was going to capture the imaginations of students, no matter their age, then I was in the wrong job. So I began to think and learn a lot more about motivating learners.

Dear Arnold,

It was two weeks into the school year and there you were in the office, pants down by your knees, no backpack and the biggest grin stretched across your face. When you asked me if I was your teacher and I said yes, you wrapped both tiny arms around my belly and gave me the biggest hug any skinny fourth grader had ever given me. As we walked to the classroom, you eagerly asking questions, I thought about how lucky I was to have you in my room since you had that great big smile, if only your pants weren't so close to your knees.

The class invited you in, they were used to kids coming in from other cities and also fell under the spell of your smile. Introductions were made, tentative friendships were formed. Then one day, you started yelling. You were so mad, I had never seen a skinny little child scream so loud and so fiercely standing up for what you thought was an injustice. Pulling you out into the hallway, I calmed you down and soon that big grin came right on back.

It was like a bubble had burst that day. The grin was hidden away and the anger and the need to fight for yourself became a frequent visitor. And yet, you never were angry at me. I never felt threatened even when other teachers pointed to my growing belly and asked how I felt safe in my room. I tried to explain to them that you were just being loud, venting a bit, and that all that screaming really was just for show, a way for you to fight for yourself as you had had to do so many times before.

Every morning you would say hello to the baby in my stomach and you would tell all the other kids about it. Every morning I would remind you to pull up your pants, until I finally got you a belt, which you then strapped around your knees so that the pants stayed right there. Almost every day I would pull you out in the hallway and remind you to just breathe, the others weren't trying to make you mad. Take a deep breath, let's talk about it.

It was time for the baby to come so I went on leave. I cried even though I knew my kids were in the best of hands. I would try to sneak by for visits with the new baby but you always spotted me from the classroom window as if you knew that today was the day I was going to stop by. You loved that little baby as much as you loved me and you told her that every time you held her. I noticed you now had sticker charts and reminders of anger management strategies and that your grades were so bad. And yet, when I walked in that door you told me about the good things. "See Mrs. Ripp, I got a C on this paper." "See Mrs. Ripp, I did this." Your pride could not be taken away.

I came back from leave and you were the first one down to my room. That big old hug came out again and you mentioned how much easier it was to hug me now. Later that afternoon, that angry little boy was there again, yelling so loud for my attention. Your lungs must have gotten bigger in the 12 weeks I was gone because I had never heard such a noise come from such a tiny child. Just breathe, it will be alright.

The school year started winding down and we still battled with your demons. I could read all of your signs. Your fist closing, your quicker breaths, your eyes darting from place to place. I knew when that voice would come back and I knew that you weren't mad at me; you were just mad at the world. And the world sometimes seemed to be mad right back at you. That final day when we said goodbye, you cried sitting under your old desk. You looked up and asked me, "But Mrs. Ripp, what am I supposed to do?" I had no answer, so I simply hugged you one more time and cried with you.

All summer I thought about you and tried to contact you, with no luck. When another year started I was told you had moved again and would not be back to my school. I just hoped and wished that I had given you enough reminders to breathe, calm down, it's not you against the world; it's us against the world.

I still look for you whenever I find myself in a big crowd of kids. Hoping that from somewhere in the middle of all those little bodies, one set of skinny arms will reach out and hug me and say "Mrs. Ripp, where did you go?" And I would tell you, "Nowhere, I am right here if you need me." Arnold, I am still right here.

My Lessons in Motivation

Here is what I know about motivation from shifting my own teaching practice:

- **Choice matters.** When students choose not just what they will do for a project but also what they would like to learn about (within some boundaries), *you get buy-in*. This continues to be one of the most simple and exciting realizations I have experienced.

- **Motivation is contagious.** When one student gets excited and has an opportunity to share that enthusiasm, the contagion spreads. My students get to blog about projects, we have huddles where we share, and we are a bit louder than we used to be. But guess what? Those loud noises are usually indicators that my students are super excited about something inside those boundaries I mentioned.

- **Punishment/reward systems stifle learning.** This short-term approach to motivation proved to be more harmful than helpful. It created a toxic learning atmosphere. Now we have class parties when we feel we want one. I have lunch with students when we can. No one is excluded from anything within the classroom.

- **Be excited yourself.** The fastest way for kids to lose interest is if you are bored. I faced up to the fact that I hated some of the things I taught and how I taught them (goodbye grammar packets). Something had to change. Now my students joke about how I almost always introduce something new with "I am so excited to do this . . ."

- **Consider outside factors.** Some students have a lot more on their plates than we could ever fully imagine. We need to ask questions, get to know our students, and be a listening ear. When my husband lost his job, it was hard for me to be excited about everyday life. I was too busy worrying. I understand how outside worry can influence the way we function within our school. I'm sure you do, too.

- **Manage and guide what's in front of you.** We will never be able to control what our students go home to, but we sure can guide what happens in the room. Good teachers choose to create a caring environment where all students feel safe. Students let their guards down and feel it is okay to work hard and have fun. It's the first essential step toward building a learning community.

Motivation in the middle school seems to be entirely different than motivation in the elementary classroom, yet I have found many similarities between the two settings. I have more frequent conversations in the middle school classroom about motivation than I have ever had before, because the habits I am fighting have been ingrained longer. Students also feel more overwhelmed trying to manage multiple teaching styles and expectations, which can lead to shutdown behavior. I need to be more tapped into what they are facing outside of my classroom so I know what I am battling with. The biggest factor in declining motivation, though, has been when students don't see the point of something and are just doing it to get it done. This has been one of my biggest barriers to work around, so having an authentic purpose that is larger than the teacher becomes vital. Student buy-in from the beginning is a must, as is student ownership and control. The reason why some projects I have attempted in my seventh grade classroom have been successful and others have not boils down to what state of mind the students were in. Having the continued conversation about purpose, choice, and how to create exciting learning opportunities is a must for all students, but especially in the middle school years.

Common or Not—The Standards Are Always There

"Teachers need to be more enthusiastic and not stay on the same topic for a month."—Paige P.

I remember the days of clutching my science curriculum in one hand while trying to write on the board with the other. Always casting glances at the script—what was I supposed to say next? And it wasn't just science, it was pretty much all of my lessons. I'd read from the paper and try to make it sound like I knew what I was talking about.

It was not lack of preparation but lack of confidence that haunted me. I thought the curriculum materials said it best, so rather than exerting ownership of the lesson, I would adopt the curriculum writers' language as my own. I tried to render it in natural speech, but as anyone who has ever taught this way knows, if you haven't thought something through in your own words, you will sound contrived and fake.

The consequence? Students will more likely tune out or lose interest, and you will look less authentic. No matter how well prepared you may be, if the words don't match you and your personality, the students will be less inclined to invest their time in the lesson.

Then: Watch Me as I Read This Aloud to You

"The chance to set up your education in the way you want is good. We need to be able to know who we learn best and then apply that to all of our school things."

—Elle R.

As any new teacher knows, this take-and-read instructional strategy is part of surviving the first year. We borrow others' lesson plans or scripts and try to make them our own. Often, we are barely treading water, enjoying the exhilarating ride (mostly) but often not knowing when we will catch our breath or actually have time to think something through. Yet, it has also become the veteran teachers' life as new curriculum replaces old ideas, often Common Core–aligned with lengthy scripts to follow and little room to figure out how to put it into our own language. With every change, a new curriculum to master, pull apart, and make work for our distinct population.

Even so, I wish I'd had the guts that first year to go out on my own a little bit. To trust myself more to deliver a good lesson—to begin asserting my own identity as a teacher who means to be great. The biggest barriers were confidence and time, of course, but I see now that I could have allowed myself to believe there was a better way. I didn't have to embrace all the advice that began: "Oh, you poor first year teacher; you'll be lucky to survive, much less succeed. Just hang on tight." If only it had occurred to me that I might let the students add their voice to how we would learn something. If only I had thought about what would have worked for me when I was a student.

To a large degree, I was also a captive of elementary school culture. We tend to steer away from anything too crazy in the lower grades. We hear about new ways of doing things and often think that if we only taught in middle school or high school, then those ideas would work. I was no different. I was aware that there were different ways of teaching—methods that didn't center around the teacher—but I thought that since I taught fourth grade, my students were not ready for that level of freedom. They needed teacher-provided structure and a firm, controlling hand as we marched through the standards and curriculum provided from on high. Now as a middle school teacher, I see the pervasiveness of the destructive thinking we tend to engage in when thinking of change. Now rather than worry about the age of my students, I worry about the pressure associated with being a middle school teacher, wishing for more freedom like I had in the elementary schools; if only we didn't have so little time and so much to cover.

I was wrong, of course. Students as young as kindergarten can thrive greatly in an environment that allows them choice and ownership of learning. We teachers just have to have the courage to actually try it with them and give it time to grow.

Now: It's All About the Students

Exit Poll

"Teachers should ask questions like Mrs. Ripp does like ask for feedback on what we are doing and how we feel about something."

—Aiden F.

I didn't transform my teaching overnight. I began by doing some things a little differently and watching to see what happened. There was a lot of experimentation and keeping my fingers crossed. I would concoct an idea, present it to the students, wait for their feedback. Then we'd make adjustments and keep moving forward. I didn't label what we were doing. I didn't know a label existed. Now I understand that I was attempting (in my own awkward way) to create a more student-centered or student-driven learning environment and to personalize our learning. But in the beginning it was truly the "Let's try it and see if it works" philosophy, which is what I encourage you to do now. Don't worry so much about what you are doing is called; don't worry so much about finding a system that you can prescribe to. Focus instead on change and embracing that you are on a journey to become a better teacher. Focus instead on that you are trying to create a passionate learning environment, where students feel valued and trusted. So adopt the "let's try" approach and trust yourself.

There's something incredibly life affirming about not being sure exactly the direction your teaching and learning is going to take and only knowing where it will end. Often when I share this sense of exhilaration with other educators, they think I am either (a) delusional or (b) that I must teach in a world that is not dictated by standards. While I may be guilty of being very optimistic, I teach in Wisconsin, in a public school that has to follow all the rules and regulations that public schools across America are following.

So when people wonder whether I have standards to meet, I can guarantee you that I have more standards than I know what to do with! Yet that hasn't stopped me from changing the way I teach, and it should never be a barrier. Some may feel that the standards or curriculum being cast upon us and our students stifle any form of creativity. I don't agree. While these things certainly establish limits, I believe we have to find our own freedom and creativity within them.

> Some may feel that the standards or curriculum being cast upon us and our students stifle any form of creativity. I don't agree. While these things certainly establish limits, I believe we have to find our own freedom and creativity within them.

Uncommon Teaching Inside the Common Core

I always start at the end. When I look at the standards, be they Common Core or district, I first want to know where we are going. I would love total freedom (although that wasn't always the case), but I know there are certain concepts, skills, and content that I have to address. I may have had textbooks that tell me what to teach, but they do not tell me *how* to teach. I may have had to follow a prescribed science curriculum, but that does not mean we cannot do the experiment and then add our own investigations.

I know that time is short for all of us, but we must find the opportunities within our curriculum to let students explore. In science, I looked at the unit's end goal and work backwards from there. One year, while studying crayfish, I knew the end goals were for students to understand the crayfish life cycle and gain a deeper respect for living creatures. Those are very broad goals, which is wonderful for this type of learning.

I asked the students how they would like to reach these goals, and through discussion they decided to create a crayfish documentary for other students to view. We decided upon a mutual timeline, and off they went down a bumpy but spectacular road. In the end, my students wrote, directed, and filmed a crayfish documentary that told me better than any test how much they knew about their science subject.

And guess what? It took the same time as the lessons proposed in the curriculum, and students were engaged the whole way through. More than that, they were not simply consuming information but problem solving—a skill we're expected to nurture and promote. With everything we teach, we should be looking for opportunities to lead our students beyond the basic standards and learning objectives, to a place where they find learning in its truest sense: something born out of curiosity and wonder; something seldom found in the "have to finish this today" environment of the pacing guide.

I realize it's not always possible to have our students roam so free. But even our most dictated curriculum can be manipulated in ways that allow us room to explore and create. We have to know our end goals, or standards, so that we can think backwards and try to visualize the most exciting path to getting there.

My best bit of advice about this: don't plan alone if you can help it. I try to reach out to my incredible colleagues, but I also reach out to my students. I cannot count the times they have taken my so-so idea and turned it into something so much richer. Let the kids own the learning and you will never have to beg them to engage. Don't shoot down ideas just because you are not sure they will work. Allow students to practice their can-do attitudes, and let them discuss expectations as well. When something doesn't work, talk about why. Make the accountability authentic rather than teacher-imposed.

"Today Is All About Innovation"

In 2010, through Twitter and my virtual colleague Josh Stumpenhorst, I came across the term *Innovation Day*. I knew right away I'd found an idea that I had to try with my students. The concept originated as "FedEx Days" in the business world, but in schools, I love that we call it Innovation Day instead, for that is what it truly is—a whole day where students get to explore whatever they choose, create something, and deliver it (that day or the next).

The rules are simple: students have to (1) learn something, (2) work the whole day, and (3) produce a product of some kind from their learning. The first year we plunged into Innovation Day, I remember being in awe over the students splayed out on the floor, immersed in their self-chosen topic. We had students building monument replicas, creating battle scenes with toy soldiers, emulating famous painters, and even building a mini zoo created from paper. I did not have to tell anyone to stay focused, keep working, or get it done. The students were completely motivated because I got out of the way and gave weight to their ideas of what learning should be. In fact, every year it continues to be *one of the most successful days* of learning we have.

It's hard to find whole days for freestyle learning. The following year, I knew we had to take the idea of Innovation Day and break it into smaller chunks. I stumbled upon the term *Genius Hour* (again through Twitter) and a new friend, Denise Krebs. She had what I needed. Now, instead of a social studies test to see how much students had learned, I had them do a genius hour, compressing the Innovation Day concept into 60 minutes. Explore, create, and deliver—all within one hour and on one particular topic. Again, ships were built, posters made, and even various technological presentations created, all aimed at showing other students what they'd learned and were interested in. My students could not believe that this was school—that a teacher "allowed" them to really explore interesting stuff.

I still followed the standards. Nowhere did it say to lecture out of a book. In fact, Common Core advocates are urging teachers to create opportunities for students to explore and gain deeper knowledge. Mission accomplished. Curriculum covered.

Lesson Planning With the End in Mind

Now when I lesson plan, I often just reflect at first. Every few years I tend to switch positions to expand my knowledge so I feel like I am always absorbing a new and ever-changing curriculum. I have to understand where the students need to end up so that I can see where we need to start.

After some pencil-free reflection, often as I drive home, I begin to write down initial ideas. Often, there are pages of content or certain mini-lessons that I have to find a way to deliver so students have the background information they need to help me figure out our direction. When we reach this point I have usually not figured out the final product(s), but I have an idea of what we could do.

This is the place when my students enter into my plans; I have often told them where we are going and then asked them to help figure out how to get there. Sometimes, it is as simple as "We need to read and understand the following pages—how can we do this?" Other times, we may be pursuing a much larger goal (such as the ones detailed in the crayfish unit). My students never fail to come up with good ideas.

This is not to say that my ideas don't have merit—some of them really do—but the student perspective is invaluable to me. After all, they are the ones who have to work through whichever requirements we design and figure out how to show what they have learned. Why not let them contribute ideas about the best ways to get where we are going? There is also nothing wrong with leaving things a bit open-ended, to tell students what the standard says and then ask them to show their mastery. When my middle school students seem particularly burnt out, this is often the approach I take: I tell them what mastery they need to show and then offer them it as a challenge. Show me you have mastered it by a certain date—how can you do this?

Next: What You Can Do, Starting Today

"Students should have a voice in their education because I think that students might have an idea that will help other students learn more."

—Mayia K.

Start at the end. Ask yourself where you need to arrive at lesson's end or to master a standard and then figure out the essential knowledge that students should uncover along the way. Keep your answers front and center throughout the process so that you know whether the path your learning community is taking is getting you there.

Ask the students as you plan. How would they like to learn something? Again, in the beginning it will take some time to have these types of discussions. Often students are not used to being asked to think this way, and they may not know how to respond. Model the conversation and then take their ideas into account. If you do not like any of their ideas try to help them come up with better ones. There should always be something you can use. And students will get better at doing this over time.

Let them think about it. Just as you need to think about lessons, it's okay to give them some "brain time" to reflect on what they would like to do.

At the end of the year, I like to have a culminating writing project that is combined with a created component. I often foreshadow it a month before we start it. The reason is simple: students need time to figure out what they would like to create that's both true to themselves and adequate to meet our goals. Because we start preparing our minds for this early, students do not feel rushed to settle on a project type (from a list of suggestions), and they also have time to dream up something original. This leads to better engagement and much better projects.

Give it time. Both you and your students need time. I sometimes get dejected when an idea doesn't work right away, but later realize that it can work or it just needs tweaking. This shared planning of the learning experience may be a completely new process to you or your students, so I think it is vital to dedicate enough class time to get it started well.

Plant the seeds of ownership early. Throughout the first week of school, I am already encouraging students to speak up and add their ideas to the classroom. By promoting this early on, students get used to being part of the discussion and have an easier time migrating from (for example) a discussion of classroom norms to actual curriculum.

Be prepared for faltering and failure. Even with the best intentions, and even when we follow a script, sometimes lessons do not work. So be prepared in case the discussion or project does not go where it needs to and try to steer it back before it is too late. If you find out too late, then make it into a learning opportunity. In my classroom, when something doesn't go as we had hoped, we always reconvene and pick it apart. Some of our best learning moments come from these student-led but teacher-guided discussions. Don't despair over perceived failure, even the most epic implosions have slivers of genius that can be salvaged. You do not always have to throw everything out when something doesn't work. Allow the ideas to simmer for a while and then see what is worth keeping.

Know your standards. You have to pick them apart to make sure you are covering them, so even though they may seem like the dullest reading you could possibly find, you should still be familiar with them. Yet, it is bigger than the Common Core or other of the big standards. In my seventh grade classroom we have 10 English-centered standards (based off of the Common Core) to master for the year. The students have deconstructed them in class and we have them all posted in their language. Students understand them and take ownership over them, and can thus evolve in a way as learners that makes sense.

Plot out the learning long-term. I am still getting the swing of this, but my dream is to be able to look at my year through big goals rather than mini-lessons. That way, I know that we are always on the correct path for the year, and not just for the unit. Yet, this does not mean to plan out the year. I have to adapt and adopt new ways of teaching every single week as my students either evolve or need more scaffolding. Yet, everything I do has to tie into a larger goal of creating passionate readers and writers.

Be open. Your classroom learning environment may work in a different way than others around you, so be open to discussion. In fact, when it comes to parents and administrators, you should be initiating the conversation. It is always much easier to gain understanding and acceptance for a different approach if others know you are still doing your job.

Give students opportunity for leadership. I switched to student-led parent conferences three years ago and have loved seeing students take ownership of their learning and their goals. Parents feel informed, and we start a dialogue rather than have me deciding everything. For more information on student-led conferences, see the appendix.

While the standards may change based on where you are and what you teach, in the end, we will always have some form of standards to teach to. What we need to do as teachers is to pull those standards apart, find your own essence as a teacher, and then put them back together throughout the year with your students in a meaningful way. While we may feel that education is always changing, remember to also get excited about some of those changes, much like we get excited at the beginning of a new year. Don't confuse that excitement for the new, though, with the need to throw everything "old" out. In this process of change, of infusing passion into your classroom again, allow yourself to keep the tried and true. To keep the "you" in the new. To keep what has worked as well. Although new ideas seem like they will fix everything, or at the very least make it all even better, your old ideas also still have value. Although new is shiny, exciting, and oh-so tantalizing, some of our old thoughts still work.

> While we may feel that education is always changing, remember to also get excited about some of those changes, much like we get excited at the beginning of a new year. Don't confuse that excitement for the new, though, with the need to throw everything "old" out.

This is not to say that new is always bad, but I think we get caught up in wanting to change everything at the start of every year or with every new book we read, rather than focusing on a few things. It seems we make these new-year resolutions about how this will be the year when we will finally become a perfect teacher, and then forget to give ourselves a break. We tend to forget that to create new habits takes a lot of work, takes a lot of energy, and that we have to also preserve ourselves in the crazy life as educators.

So go ahead: get excited, dream up the new, but don't forget about the old things that worked. About the old ideas that were new once. Some will still work. Parts of you will still work, even as you start a new way of teaching.

We have all been in this situation, it seems: surrounded by negative people whose only joy in life seems to be finding something to complain about. Those teachers who cannot wait to share how terribly a child did, those teachers who cannot wait to discuss how awful a new initiative will be, or even just how overwhelmed they feel. And you know what, at some point we have probably all been one of those teachers. I know I was! And we usually don't even know it.

So what can we do if we find ourselves surrounded by the negative? How do you move beyond it, inspire change, but not look like you are complaining yourself?

First idea is to reflect: are you adding to the negative? Are you getting sucked into the conversations? Are you adding fuel to the fire? Misery loves company. It is so easy to get wrapped up in a juicy story about a demanding parent or how there was another stupid idea proposed. If you are even a little bit guilty of participating in these conversations, stop. Catch yourself in the act and change your own direction. Change your narrative and share the positive. This doesn't mean you cannot discuss hard situations, just change the way you phrase them.

Second idea: change the immediate conversation. So if someone starts to complain, see if you can spin it in a positive way. If a child is being discussed, highlight something positive. If you see a conversation turning into something that will not benefit you and you cannot change it, you also have the right to walk away. Even if you like the person speaking, nothing says you have to be a part of it. Sometimes our actions speak louder than words.

Third idea: acknowledge the negative and then try to problem-solve. If the negative continues to surround you, acknowledge it because sometimes people don't even know they are doing it. This doesn't mean calling them out in an uncomfortable way, but just acknowledging that what they are saying seems to be bothering them and if they are looking for someone to problem-solve with. We all have days where we need to release some of the energy that seems to be haunting us; sometimes discussing it is our way of reaching out to work through it. So offer to be that person, withhold judgment, and try to alleviate the negative.

Fourth idea: look for the positive. Sometimes our own perception makes a person seem much more negative than he or she really is. Are you seeing him or her as a whole person or just someone who complains? Make sure your own thoughts aren't clouding a situation.

Fifth idea: get to know them more. We don't always know what is going on in someone's life. Sometimes when they are complaining about little things it may be an indicator that their life outside of school is stressful right now. I know I have a much lower tolerance for anything when I am too busy outside of work or not sleeping well because of stress. So if someone seems to take a turn toward the worse, see if you can find out what is going on. Express your concern, be there as a friend, and remember to see her or him as a human being. We all have bad days. We all have moments where we are at our lowest.

No one comes to work meaning to be the negative force; no one walks into a social situation hoping to change it into a vent fest. Sometimes it just happens. Sometimes life gets the better of us and we don't know that we are "that" person. When all else fails, you just have to shrug it off. Continue to be a positive force for good; continue to keep yourself in check; continue to be aware of what you put out in the world. We are not able to change other people, but we can change the environment we teach in in small ways. What do you do to diffuse the negative?

Homework, Routines, and a Whole Lot of Paper

"Students should not have homework unless they need it. When a student does not understand or needs more practice this is the time to assign individualized homework." —Kyle U.

As I prepared my first Orientation Day slideshow as a new teacher, I knew I had to fill in homework expectations, including how much time students and parents should commit to every night. Since it was my first year, I had no idea what the curriculum expectations were, so I relied on the old formula of 10 minutes times the grade of the child: fourth graders would have a minimum 40 minutes of homework every night.

Now this is what my brain should have thought: "Wait a minute Pernille, 40 minutes of homework a night?! Plus 20 minutes of expected reading with parent initials? And a book report every six weeks? And math tests every three weeks?" Not to mention science and social studies quizzes, which really are tests with a friendlier name, plus don't get me started on the spelling quizzes as well.

I didn't think those thoughts, and the rest, as they say, is history. My fourth grade students had homework coming out of both ears because that is what I thought teachers did—assign work! Forty minutes seemed fair and reasonable, and why shouldn't it be? Aren't we in the business of making students accountable and responsible? Aren't we teaching them how to be effective workers and preparing them for the real world?

The problem? Homework is really not thoughtful when you just assign to check off a box or follow a guideline for how many minutes students should work outside of school. Homework then becomes a brainless act of repetition, not the metacognitive contemplation that we all should be striving for. Homework becomes the incessant chore we all seem so hellbent on making it.

I know we are trying to raise responsible children, but is homework really the only way we can do this? Can we not accomplish those same goals of responsibility, time management, and good work habits without an insane amount of homework? Can we consider whether we have the right to infringe on students' lives outside of class up to an hour or more every night? Haven't students already given us seven to eight hours of work during the day? There is a better way.

Then: I Think I Worksheeted Them to Death

"Teachers should not assign homework because we already learn enough in class."

—Zack D.

I never used to hate homework. Worksheets and assignments to be completed at home were just a part of teaching. You lecture, you have students participate by raising their hands to supply an answer, and then you assign the homework. Every class gets its own—weekends mean I can assign more—and vacations are meant for longer projects. The more free time they have, the more time they have to work.

As a child, I rebelled against homework, often forgetting or simply not caring to do the task assigned. Yet when I became a teacher I assigned it almost every day. I gave little thought to whether students could accurately accomplish it. I simply mandated it because I thought I had to. In fact, for their birthdays they would receive a "no homework" pass that they could use for one assignment that had to be approved by me. They were ecstatic and that should have been a huge clue.

One night I told my husband that I knew exactly which kids would hand in their assignment with some "help" from their parents, which kids would hand in something half finished, and which kids would never hand it in at all, regardless of any threats I threw in their direction. I knew something wasn't right. Homework was meant to be about practice and gaining proficiency, yet my students abhorred most of it. They either went through the motions to complete it or offered creative reasons why they hadn't, much like I did myself as a child.

Upon further reflection, I also knew which students would not be able to complete the work regardless of their intentions or how much help I gave them at school; they simply did not have the skills or resources needed to finish it at home. Homework completion and the punishments and rewards tied to it were a part of the great divide in my classroom—another rote requirement that kept us from becoming a united group of invested learners.

My *Ahas* About Homework

Despite these new understandings, giving up homework seemed somehow irresponsible. It was expected of me, part of the unspoken rules of teaching. Parents looked for it, and students knew it was coming. I was not sure I had the courage to stop the assignments. Then I realized several things:

◆ Homework can become an excuse for the stuff we just don't get to in class, which certainly had been part of my teaching method. When teachers do this, do we hope they'll just figure that stuff out? If truncated lessons are the source of our homework assignments, then we need to look at how we spend the time we have with students. If we know the goal of the lesson, we need to get to it.

◆ Another realization had to do with the idea that most homework is practice. Some kids will take five minutes to do it. That means they are already secure in the concept. Some will take 30 minutes with parent help. That may or may not be meaningful. Others will never finish because they're not prepared to practice alone. If we do not equip a student with the knowledge and confidence needed to complete the homework, then we should not assign it. We can certainly differentiate the work, but why send it home in the first place if few of our students will benefit from it?

◆ Homework steals time from childhood for little good reason. I came across research suggesting that, particularly at the elementary level, most homework does not boost achievement. I started to see homework for what it really was: a deterrent for children to pursue their lives outside of school. We ask students to do their very best for the seven-plus hours we have them within our schoolhouse walls, and then we ask for another hour or more after they leave us. Couple that with lengthy school bus rides here in America, and there simply is not much time left for a kid to be a kid.

Instead of assigning more work for them, I began to think, give them the time to explore, read, play, or just relax. Let them wind down from the imposed rigor of school so that perhaps they'll return excited rather than exhausted. Why not cherish that which is childhood? It is only lived once, and there will be plenty of time later for worksheets and other inane tasks imposed on us by adults.

◆ Another limitation of most homework is that it does not always fit the learning. As I progressed toward more student-created learning explorations, I quickly realized that most worksheets (a frequent homework task) had no place in my classroom. Simply said, not all skills that are taught transfer onto paper well, particularly in younger grades. Math can lend itself well to paper exercises, but why assign three pages if student understanding can be accomplished through a few problems? Before we assign homework, and steal that time from childhood, we have to put ourselves to a serious test: does it really afford students a way to learn or demonstrate their learning that could not be accomplished within the school day?

◆ There are myriad shades of homework. Some teachers have students venture into their communities as an extension of classroom studies. Many others ask students to read outside of school. This purposeful activity is not what I fight against; what I oppose is homework for the sake of homework—homework as a habit. If we decide students should have assignments outside of school, our kids should be engaging in meaningful learning experiences that will help them grow not just as learners, but as people.

Now: Explore, Create, Dream, and Fail

"I believe that in school work is important but I also think some kids might need a little more practice than others. On the other hand, we are in school for about seven hours and I feel that the extra free time in the afternoons when we would be doing our homework we could be using that time with our families."

—Isabel O.

I once believed that homework taught time management and responsibility, and accurately showed what students knew. Now I know that homework can be done by parents, that the child who struggles in class will struggle at home, and that I have no right to take more of my students' time. Time management, responsibility, and practice can be taught in school if we control our curriculum and set up effective learning environments. When we move away from the "drill and kill" approach to teaching, we should also move away from traditional homework assignment. Yet the path to a homework-free classroom is not clear cut.

Even though I made the decision several years ago to eliminate most of my homework, doing so in our test-obsessed, standards-driven educational environment proved difficult. The idea makes great sense on paper, and I wish I could say that my students have no homework whatsoever, but that would not be the truth. They have limited homework because there are some things I have not figured out how to get around just yet.

Nevertheless, my focus on limiting homework for the past five years and more has given me some valuable insight and helped me sharpen my practice.

> I once believed that homework taught time management and responsibility, and accurately showed what students knew. Now I know that homework can be done by parents, that the child who struggles in class will struggle at home, and that I have no right to take more of my students' time.

How I Limit Homework

- ◆ A textbook may be Common Core–aligned without achieving more focused instruction. It may just mean there are more pages to get through. Case in point: the daily expectations in the math curriculum I taught went from an average of three notebook/journal pages to five. I had to pick and choose what was presented to students as we tried to get through it all and still have time for me to meet with students for remediation. While this required extra planning and a deeper knowledge of the standards I was supposed to be adhering to, it was worth it for me. Even so, on many days there were still math pages to go through at home. I did my very best, by differentiating assignments, to avoid frustration by asking students to only complete math problems where they have grasped the essentials.

- ◆ In some schools, there may not be enough time for independent reading. There have been years like that for me, when I had to ask my students to read outside of class as well. Our compromise was that I did not monitor what they read or whether they read as much as I asked of them. It was an honor system. Fortunately, our district has now given us more literacy time and moved us to a workshop model.

- ◆ Some students will struggle with getting things finished, even if class time is given. Even in my much more engaging classroom, students who face learning hurdles (e.g., attention problems) or even just have motivation issues still end up with late work. Some students will always struggle with deadlines and will also struggle with how to manage their time in school. To keep schoolwork from lapping over into homework too often, it becomes part of my teaching to show these students how to be successful time managers and self-starters. That means we map out when we are working on things, we create a plan for what we are working on when, and we discuss in small groups how those plans are going. None of this takes very long, not all students need it, but those that do benefit greatly.

◆ Taking recess away used to be my most-often used punishment for not doing homework, even though I have never liked denying children the chance to play. It continues to be against my beliefs, but there are times when I have to ask children to sacrifice part of their recess time. Children can get so behind or so lackadaisical about getting work done and using their time wisely that they have to stay in so we can work through it together. Once they are done with the work, out they go.

◆ Some parents or administrators will not understand why homework is generally not worthwhile; after all, they suffered through it just fine. (Others will despise it more than I do.) The point is this: I need to communicate what I'm doing and why I'm doing it; otherwise, parents or administrators may think I am simply being lazy or crazy and press for more.

◆ In a classroom with limited homework, there has to be a lot of talking. On any given day, I spend most of my time in conversation with students about their learning. Often our conversations allow me to make assessments based on what they are mastering and what they are still struggling with. I can adjust my teaching to fit their needs. If I find that limited homework is necessary, I have a lot of knowledge about what and why.

Since becoming a middle school teacher in a district that does not tie final grades in with homework, nor require it, it has been interesting to see what can happen to the whole notion of homework. There seems to be a distinct difference in how students tackle homework: some do it to the best of their ability, diligently working through everything we ask them to do; some rush through it and hand it in, never to look at it again even though I teach in a district with a retake policy in place; and finally you have those that will never do it, no matter how much they need the practice. So basically, even in a district where homework is only viewed as practice and is not used as a way to punish students, the same problems surround it. While I continue to only ask my students to read 20 minutes a night, my homework philosophy still holds: work hard in our classroom and you should have to spend minimal time on English outside of school. Waste your time and the work you have not completed now has to be done at a different time. This means that I have students with homework loads, while others may not have anything. I make sure that those students who are struggling have my support during study hall or other times, I modify as needed, and try to provide the practice that students need within class. Yes, it is hard when you teach in 45-minute blocks. Yes, sometimes I wish I could tell students to just do it at home and come to school prepared to discuss. And yet, I would never go back to assigning the homework I used to. My students know I work hard to keep English to the 45 minutes we have every day, so they work hard in return.

Our curriculum load is heavy and can seem near impossible to get through in the time available, so I battle the homework issue every day. I am getting better every year, though, as I become wiser about how my students can navigate the learning goals and show me they have mastered them in the least amount of time necessary. I hardly ever use worksheets outside of class. If we have to show mastery we do it within class time as much as we can, and we do much more project-based learning with student- and teacher-determined learning goals.

> I hardly ever use worksheets outside of class. If we have to show mastery we do it within class time as much as we can, and we do much more project-based learning with student- and teacher-determined learning goals.

I do not believe that homework is the best way we can teach students responsibility or independent work skills. But to do it you have to be willing to tear apart your curriculum, tear apart your expectations of what a finished product looks like, and discover what your students can actually accomplish. Not easy, but worth it in the end.

Since homework is a mainstay of school, I decided I would ask my students an innocent question: "Should teachers assign homework? Why or why not?" Based on my own philosophical beliefs, I thought the answer would be a resounding no, yet my students surprised me with their nuanced answers. It is not that they are against all homework, they simply ask that teachers keep a few things in mind before they assign it.

⟶ **They wish teachers knew just how busy they are.** That we ask them to live balanced lives that involve sports, family, friends, and sleeping, yet assign hours of work that pushes their bedtime later and later. They cannot fit everything in, even though they try.

⟶ **They wish teachers knew just how stressed they are.** That they feel like our expectations are through the roof at all times, but sometimes they are bound to mess up, and can we make that okay as well? Can it be okay to forget once in a while or to not get it all right?

—→ **They wish teachers knew that they don't always need the practice.** That homework should be for those kids that don't quite get it, not assume a need for everyone, and that those that really don't get it won't get it after they do the homework. That they need help in school instead.

—→ **They wish teachers knew how much we all assign.** That we spoke to one another more so that we see that our class may not assign a lot, but when you add each class together, it is now hours of work, not just a little bit of time.

—→ **They wish teachers knew that they have worked really hard in school and wish they could have a break.** That homework on some days is okay but it doesn't need to be every day. Nor does it need to be over the holidays. That they get we have a lot to cover but can they promise us to work hard in school in exchange for time off from school?

—→ **Finally, they wish teachers actually did their own homework.** That they tried the assignments so they could see how difficult or confusing they may be. That they worked through it with kids, not in a pretend way, but really, and then shared their own learning with students. That teachers truly felt what it means to live the life of a student, along with the pressure of homework, to understand why homework continues to be a problem for some.

Please keep the wishes of my students, and I am sure many students, in mind as you look for ways you can change your own homework practice.

Next: What You Can Do Starting Today

"I think that the only time we should get homework is if we didn't use our time wisely and didn't get it done."

—Maiya K.

Eliminating or limiting homework can be a frightening endeavor. We're going up against one of the most institutionalized and ingrained parts of our educational system. Yet, as many teachers worldwide have shown, it is not impossible. Reducing or eliminating homework is very much dependent on an individual teacher's situation. Here are my suggestions about how to get started:

1. **Do your research first.**
   If you plan on being the only teacher (or one of a few) to not assign homework, you have to know your reasons why. A great place to start is with Alfie Kohn's book *The Homework Myth;* it contains much of the

relevant research needed for you to make your stand. Also do some soul searching. My decision to limit homework was not just based on my own personal belief about the sanctity of family time and student accomplishment, but also propelled on by the research that indicates it makes no difference in achievement.

2. **Start a conversation with your administrators.**
   If they are not on-board with you, it is going to be an uphill battle. Make sure that you are not in violation of policy. Transparency is key. Start the conversation so that they can understand and approve your plan.

3. **Decide how else students can show off their learning.**
   This goes hand in hand with moving toward a more student-directed/personalized learning environment, as well as being project based; worksheets seem to disappear in classrooms that promote this type of learning. There are many ways to assess student learning that can work within the time constraints of the day—and not just testing.

4. **Remove all punishment aspects from homework.**
   It is important to move away from using homework as a way to control students and realize that if homework is indeed for practice purposes then it should not be graded, and students should not be punished if it is not completed. Whole districts, such as the Oregon School District in Wisconsin where I teach, have implemented homework policies where it is practice, not to be tied in with a final grade, meaning it is actually possible to do.

5. **Remove grading from homework.**
   While giving up grading is discussed more thoroughly in Chapter 10, one way to compromise in a school culture that dictates homework is to remove the grading aspect. If you are creating learning opportunities that are more hands-on, this step should be a natural extension. Homework should be used to meet instructional needs, not measure student accomplishments.

6. **Move away from a snapshot mentality.**
   Most homework (like tests) is used as a snapshot of what the student knows at that moment in time. In a more student-centered classroom, we should focus on overall knowledge and intellectual

growth, not snapshots. Strive to create learning opportunities that show growth over time as well as student ownership. Also: allowing for re-dos when children need another chance to do the work is vital to their progression as learners. And remember that the re-do can be in the shape of a conversation rather than a project. Or homework. You can limit the time frame of the re-do/re-take to two weeks as an example so that students have a sense of when they should have mastered it.

7. **Purge the worksheets.**
This is my most literal suggestion. I threw away most of my worksheets and refused (to myself) to make more copies of them. This way, I have to come up with a different way to assess rather than just open up my file cabinet at the last minute.

8. **Involve parents.**
Too often decisions regarding students are made without the input of parents. Be upfront about your decision to cut or limit homework and then explain why. Invite parents to question and discuss this with you at conferences, and always keep an open line of communication regarding this or any other policy you may have.

9. **Give it time and allow yourself leeway.**
Perhaps you cannot get as much eliminated as you had envisioned, but that does not mean you have failed. It simply means it is a work in progress, so continue to invest the time in cutting homework back.

10. **Get connected.**
Right away. You are not the only one trying this, I promise, so connect with others attempting to do it as well. Get online and find colleagues via Google +, Twitter, Facebook, or whichever social media site you gravitate toward and ask them questions. Find a colleague locally that shares some of the same thoughts. I write online about my quest to give up homework because I want to show others that it is possible. Use other people as your guiding posts and inspiration; you will be able to add much more to the conversation than you might think.

In the end, if you have to assign homework, please only do so when it is meaningful, relevant, and doable for the child. It should not be assigned because we feel the need to cover more material. It should not be assigned when we know a child will struggle through it. It should not be assigned over vacations, nor between grade levels. Homework should be limited to when a child truly needs the practice, can do it, and will grow from it, and even then we must be selective in what we assign. The biggest thing I have learned in my struggles with homework and trying to limit it is that it is pervasive in most cultures, so as parents and teachers we must fight it when our child our students do not need it. We must remember that all children are on different learning journeys and thus do not need the same things. We know this innately with our curriculum; it is time we extend that to our homework practices.

10

How Grading Destroys Curiosity

"I know I'm better than the letter grades teachers give me." —David B.

Four times a year, I have a mini-breakdown. It always begins when I am about to start report cards. Being a teacher who doesn't believe in grades for assessment but would rather do feedback, I always struggle. How do I put into words all of the things that I have seen my students do in in the last few months? How do I quantify how they have grown? There just seems to be so many things a report card doesn't tell us, even if it is standards based.

It doesn't tell the story of the child who has worked so hard every day yet has made little academic progress. It doesn't tell the story of the boy who hated to read and now has read two books this month. Or the story of the child who thinks he is the world's worst writer but did an assignment all on his own. Or the girl who struggles with self esteem and thus doesn't want to shine a light on herself even though she should. Or the child who knows everything there is about DNA but doesn't know his letter sounds.

It doesn't tell the story of so many children who know more than their minds let them show. Or even the story of the teacher who tries every day to get these kids to believe in themselves and their ability to change the world.

Which grade do I assign all of that?

Then: I Was Queen of the "F"

"Grades don't say how much I learned, it is just an opinion. People can't say how much I learned and how hard I tried because I am the only one who knows that."

—Brooke S.

I used to be obsessed with grading. I was the queen of the "F." If students weren't handing in their homework, I whipped out my trusty calculator and showed them exactly what would happen to their grade average if they didn't hand it in. If students weren't paying attention, I repeated my message: you will do poorly on the test and get a big fat F that will be so, so hard to overcome.

What if a child didn't behave? Just another great opportunity to drop the "F" bomb. I was not going to allow a disrespectful child to get good grades in my room. Good grades were reserved for those who knew how to do school well—sit down, be quiet, be a good student. The dreaded 60% nipped at my students' heels, just waiting to swallow them up if they ever slowed down in our academic race. We had things to do, worksheets to complete, and projects to hand in. Get on it, or that "F" is coming for you.

All this, even though I have waged a personal battle with grades all my life—from the days when I was a kid who "never applied herself" to an anxious college overachiever whose only goal was to get a 4.0 and make up for all those wasted years. I could never get my grades to fit me. They never showed my interests, my smarts, or my deficits. They were always just arbitrary numbers assigned to me on the basis of how well I could "do school." You would think, therefore, that early in my teaching career, I would have closely questioned traditional grading practices. But much like the other systems we learn in teacher college, I adopted the practice of most teachers who came before me. Figure out your grading scale and then use it every chance you get.

As a new teacher, I fiddled, I muddled, and I tweaked. My carefully crafted rubric would tell me students deserved a particular grade, and yet (I really wasn't quite so mean) it sometimes broke my heart to give it to them. My rubric didn't care whether children had done the work all on their own, or whether this was the first writing assignment they'd ever managed to finish. Nor did it care whether a child understood something or simply did not have enough time to finish.

Why was I surprised when the averages and grades I came up with never seemed to tell the story of my students' learning lives? They finished a product, received their grade, and we moved on. The grade meant we were done. I never used the grade as an opportunity to discuss their knowledge; we would do that at conference time.

In the end, grading degrades. A poor grade tells students that no matter how hard they worked, if that effort does not fit into the teacher's rubric, or vision, or plan for them, then they just wasted their time. In the grades-driven classroom, students learn that even though their parents are fighting, and they can't get their homework done because they are scared, they still pay the teacher's homework penalty, whatever that might be.

Grades tell students that even though they devour their books and can't wait to talk to somebody about them, when they forget to include the title and author on a book report, they must not be "A+" readers. Grading tells students that they may have way too much responsibility at the age of 10, but that I don't care whether they're too tired today to do their best work.

As educators, we know the many negative side effects of traditional grading and the frequent injustice it represents. We see the defeat in students' eyes when they don't get the grade they had hoped for. We see it at parent/teacher conferences when parents zero in on the bad grades, ignoring all the pluses we so meticulously planted on the report card. We see it in the kids who show off their top grades yet have no real idea of why they received them or what they indicate. The learning we have planned becomes nothing but a vehicle to produce a grade, not something to expand upon or ponder over, or get intrinsic satisfaction from accomplishing.

When I came to all these conclusions, I decided to quit grading as much as I could within the public school system.

Now: I Love My Gradeless Classroom

"What does a grade tell me about myself? Sometimes it says a lot, other times nothing. I feel sometimes if people/teachers look at some grades, they might get the wrong idea about me."

—Payton U.

I believed that grades were an accurate measure of learning. Now I know that they are subjective and misleading at best, detrimental to learning at their worst. Yet quitting grades to some means quitting expectations, and I knew I had to fight that notion if I was going to make a permanent change.

When I quit putting letter grades or percentages on my papers, I did not lower my expectations; in fact, quite the opposite happened. By removing letter grades from the final product, it ceased being exactly that: final. Now when an assignment is handed in, my students know it may not be done. It is no longer seen as an end product, but instead as another potential stepping stone in our learning journey. If a test result is mediocre they have a chance to fix it. I cannot tell you how many times I have witnessed a student look at a test paper with fresh

> When I quit putting letter grades or percentages on my papers, I did not lower my expectations; in fact, quite the opposite happened. By removing letter grades from the final product, it ceased being exactly that: final.

eyes and say "Oh!"—then erase the incorrect answer and replace it with the correct one.

I didn't quit using letter grades because I wanted to shelter my students from the "real" world. I quit because they did not spark any kind of discussion regarding the work (unless the grade was not what had been expected by parents). If an "A–" was given, I never had students wonder what they could have done better or even ask what was so great about the work they did. The grade was received, glanced at, and the product filed away, perhaps to be shared with a parent, but at some point soon to be shared with a recycling bin.

I wanted a better pathway to deeper discussions about learning, and I wanted us to be free from the ever encroaching averages that distracted us so much.

Let us be frank: it is much easier for me to grade my students than it is to properly assess them through conversations. Teachers know this. Grading means I can share a due date, collect the assignment from the students, and based upon a rubric or key I can assign their percentage and translate it into a grade.

I can do most of this in the comfort of my own home. I do not need nor want students to be present for this process. Once their grade is entered into my gradebook, I can hand the graded paper back to the children; assessment complete. I do not need to speak to them about their work because it would not change how they were graded. The grade has been entered in the official record, and it will not be changed.

I could dock them points if they handed homework in late or didn't have their name on it. I could also dock them points for messiness or lack of creativity. In the end, they would have very little feedback related to their grade and they would probably be fine with that; most kids are. Grading, it seems, is the easy way out. At least for the teacher.

Authentic Assessment Is Messy

"What does a grade tell me about myself? If I am strong at that subject or weak or maybe that we don't give a darn about it."

—Thor A.

True assessment is messy and time consuming. It involves speaking to the children about their work and their progress. You have to find the time to speak to all of them about whatever they are working on, and then you have to actually listen while they speak in order to evaluate and brainstorm together. If the project is sizable, this will not be a one-time visit either; there must be multiple check-ins. When the project is finished and handed in, you must find the time to look through it with the child. Based on your conversations all along the way, you discuss its strengths, its weaknesses, and how it could be improved. In some instances, you give it back to them to make the improvements. In the classroom where you teach more than just one class, this can be a daunting task. How do you have all of these conversations when you only see a student for perhaps 45 minutes in a day?

This process and these kinds of conversations do not translate into neat percentages that can be averaged. They do not translate well into grades because what I consider "accomplished" may be different from someone else's opinion of excellent work. Yet I know from experience that doing assessment this way makes you feel that you really know each child you are teaching—their knowledge, their passions, and what they need to focus on. Percentages don't tell you that.

You may think that you could never find the time to have all of these discussions with your students, particularly if you teach more than one group of children. Here you must remember that you decide what their assignments look like. You decide how time will be spent in your classroom. We have more power over how we teach than we think or admit, even with all of the standards and regulations we face. In many instances, we decide how the minutes are invested, how material is covered, and how students learn together. Isn't it time we also decide how they are assessed?

I will admit it now: Not grading is a pain! Not grading means that I can no longer assign a score, translate it into a grade, record it and forget about it. Not grading means I now have to have anecdotal evidence to back up my final grade on the report card that I still have to do. That evidence has to not only be collected, but also stored somewhere for the entire year so that I can refer back to it when I discuss student growth with anyone. And sometimes not grading means students still find a way to quantify themselves.

Not grading also means that my students have not been given a percentage-based score at any time throughout the year, so they have to understand why they get the grades they get on their report card. Not grading means that a product can take weeks before it is truly completed because a student may have to rework or revisit it in some way to achieve his or her best effort.

It is a whole lot of work to not grade in the traditional sense.

But here's the payoff: Although not grading is a lengthier process, the growth and investment I have seen in my students since abandoning traditional letter grades has surpassed even my loftiest ambitions. Now I give feedback and initiate discussions regarding their work. I point out their stellar thinking and where they need to improve something. They evaluate each other's work as well, and we have (awesome) whole-room discussions about what an accomplished product should look like. We now have student voice as part of the deliberations, which leads to a much more interesting learning environment, since they again are affirmed in the notion that their voice matters.

In the end, not assigning letter grades in my classroom has meant more open discussions regarding learning. Students no longer ask me how to get an "A" on an assignment. Why would they? Instead, we discuss what they would like to uncover and learn. As well, they can change and expand their learning goals within lengthier assignments, without risking a lower grade, and they start to uncover how they learn best.

To hear students take control of their learning, to own up to where they should have worked harder, to set up their future path for learning—wow. This is what assessment should be. I learn as much from these discussions as the students do, and I always take their feedback to heart as I reflect on my teaching practice. I am a learner alongside them, and what a powerful modeling of lifelong learning that is.

> When you teach more than 30 students, finding time for feedback is much harder, and yet it is not impossible. I have learned that I do not need to grade everything that my students hand me.

When you teach more than 30 students, finding time for feedback is much harder, and yet it is not impossible. I have learned that I do not need to grade everything that my students hand me. Instead, I often file it for them. When we get ready to assess a standard, I ask them to pick the work that shows their mastery. This way students see that the work they did was true practice and are also in control of what they would like me to assess. I often encourage them to tweak or read over what they do decide to hand me, just to see if it can grow even stronger. Students take ownership over how they are assessed and I can use all of my time deciding what they have accomplished and what they should continue to work on.

Next: What You Can Do, Starting Today

"To me grades at school are who you are. I feel like everyone is judged on their GPA and how smart they are. It's not a good thing because it makes some students feel bad about themselves at school."

—Corinne

Many paths may lead you to think about grading and how it harms learning in students. I know from experience how daunting the journey to no grades may be. Yet, there is a way to do it, and here is the path I've taken.

No Grades—Before You Start

1. **Do your research.** Since limiting grades or removing them completely can be a rather contentious act, it's important to have your facts straight. Read Alfie Kohn's work about grades and then expand to include the numerous blogs, articles, and reflections you'll find on the topic through a Google search.

2. **Think it through.** This is a bucking-the-system type of decision, so you need to be clear on why you are doing this. Providing students with more meaningful feedback: yes. Less work and more free time: no.

3. **Be practical.** What is this going to look like in your room? How will you take notes? How will you assess their learning? And then, how will you compile that all into feedback, progress reports, and perhaps even a dictated grade on a district report card?

4. **Create your goals.** All lessons have to have goals; otherwise, you will have nothing to assess. Sometimes, we are not totally sure what those goals are since a curriculum has been prescribed to us. Dig through it and find them or create your own within the standards, and then make a list or some sort of report. I was able to quickly assess through verbal Q&A whether a student was secure in something or not and then check off that goal, moving that student on to something else. I now work in a standards-based grading district, so our end goals are mastery of the standards the students have rewritten into friendlier language. Often one project will be for the practice of multiple standards and we discuss these throughout the work-time. Students know exactly what their goals are and can also choose to work beyond them.

5. **Involve the higher-ups.** I didn't have to alert my principal to what I was planning on doing, but it made my life a lot easier when I did. Some districts will not support non-grading practices without

a proper discussion, and it is important to have allies if someone questions your program or philosophy.

6. **Explain it to your families and particularly your students.** Going gradeless or limiting the amount of grades students are given should not a be a surprise to those it involves—namely students and their families. Acknowledge and celebrate that you will be working in a feedback-centered classroom. Get it out in the open and start the discussion right away with parents. Start the conversations with them so that they know you welcome open dialogue. Front load as much as possible, and be ready to prove to them that they will be more informed than they were before.

7. **Involve your students.** We tend to think we are in this alone, but nothing could be further from the truth. Involve your students in the feedback or grade discussion, since you more than likely will still be required to give a grade sometime during the year (mine was on trimester report cards). If you let students first determine their grade and then meet to discuss it with you, even this grade setting process can become part of the feedback cycle. Doing this with my students caused them to focus on the feedback rather than pine for a grade. Most of the time, their grades and mine lined up perfectly; occasionally they were much harder on themselves than I was. Either way, we figured it out together, through conversation and reflection, and they started to own their learning more.

8. **Plan for it.** Meaningful assessment does not just happen; it is planned and somehow noted. It is ongoing and cannot be trusted to memory. As I developed my methods, every day I had my trusty clipboard where I took notes, checked off progress and goals accomplished, and added anything else useful. This became my "grade book," and the days I didn't use it, all of that information was lost. Find your own system. Many teachers use Evernote or some similar technology. If you prefer, a trusty old binder will do. Whatever your system is, refine it until it works dependably for you and your students. Yet, allow yourself to not take notes on everything, not every single conversation with a student has to be recorded, nor goals set. Sometimes we need to lay down our note-taking tools and simply focus on the conversation at hand.

9. **Take your time.** Letter grades will always be easier to do because they are most often compiled from a piece of paper or a one-time presentation. Deep feedback is not so simple. This is gathered through conversations, assignments, and lots and lots of formative assessment. Give yourself time to take it all in. And do not skimp on the conversations. The conversations are the most important tool here. If you feel pressed for time, or have many students, then allow yourself to write out your thoughts for students to see. You can also use a tool like Voxer, a free walkie-talkie app that lets you record your voice and then email it to someone.

10. **Allow yourself to experiment.** See what happens when you don't give letter grades; try other forms of assessment; figure out if it works for you. Give yourself permission to see this as a work in progress. I have had several limited-grades years now and there were definitely missed opportunities in my room concerning feedback. But I know what to work on now. I also know what my goals are, how to engage students in meaningful conversation regarding their work, and also how to give them better feedback. Just like our students, we too, are learning.

11. **Most important: reach out.** Through my online PLN, I was able to engage in meaningful conversations about grading and iron out hurdles with the help of Joe Bower, Jeremy MacDonald, and Chris Wejr. I even reached out to Alfie Kohn. There are people who have done this before you, people who have survived the hard pushbacks; use them, ask them questions, and come to see that you are far from alone.

No Grades—As You Start

1. **Discover your goal.** Whether the learning goals are based on the Common Core Standards, district goals or even school outcomes, you have to figure out the goal for everything you teach. These can be large or small (do not do too many small ones, though, trust me). Then figure out what the outcome should be. What is the minimal amount of learning the students should encounter? Everything you do should have a learning goal because without it there is no point to your teaching.

2. **Determine the product.** What does it look like when students have accomplished the goal? What is "finished"? How will students show they have mastered their goal? I love to have this discussion with my students. Also, realizing that there are many different pathways to the same goal is a must. My students almost always have different ways to show mastery, where one path is a more traditional way such as a writing assignment or test, and another is their own created choice. Allowing for choice, while still providing scaffolds for those who need it, is the way we should teach every day.

3. **Determine the best assessment.** Will it be written feedback, a rubric, a conversation? Once again, ask the students what type of assessment will help them grow. How will they learn the most?

4. **Keep a record.** This has been my biggest hurdle. I have had charts, gradebook notes, relied on my faulty brain, even binders. I have even tried Google Docs and Evernote (tagging can be helpful) as a way to keep track of conversations, assessments, and anything else I think may come in handy. And while I have yet to find the perfect system, I keep coming back to binders with sheets for each student. Whatever system you end up using, find one that will make record keeping easy and accessible, suited to your personality.

5. **Communicate.** Assessment is worthless if the feedback is not properly communicated to students through a small conference or written feedback. Then make sure you communicate it to parents. The allure of letter grades is just that—the ease of communication—even though a grade can mean a hundred different things. So make sure you replace grades with plenty of communication. Give students ownership of their goals and have them write a status report, send home an email, make a phone call, just communicate somehow. While a status report sounds fancy, it is typically just a sheet of paper with the name of the student and the different projects or standards we are working on. They then do a self-evaluation, and add goals that they are working on what they have accomplished. I tweak it to make it work for where we are in the year. All students should be able to describe where they are and where they are headed, throughout the year.

No Grades—As You Implement

1. **Define your purpose.** It is important for you to know the "why" of what you are doing, so take time to soul-search. Come up with your own words that clearly explain why moving away from grades is important and then continue to reflect as you go. Devising your own evolving narrative for the "why" will help you refine your process.

2. **Stay true to you.** There are many ways to do no grades, and you have to find the one that works best for you. Perhaps that means creating other types of rubrics or feedback forms; perhaps that means having students self-assess with set guidelines.

3. **Make it work for you.** Keep it as simple as you can; you are the one using what you pull together. You know how your brain works for gathering feedback and artifacts to support student learning, so incorporate those methods into your process.

4. **Involve students.** Students, even at an elementary level, know how to set up evaluations and are surprisingly tough on themselves. I love the rich discussions that come from asking what a finished product should look like and how we can decide whether we met those goals.

5. **Explain, explain, and explain!** You will inevitably run into people who think you are nuts (right in your own school, for starters), so have your facts and reasons ready. One way to start the conversation is to be very honest in your reasoning as well as your methodology and engage in a meaningful conversation with them. I always am open to discussing all of my philosophies and actively solicit feedback about them throughout the year from other adults; this tends to diffuse any negative situations or misunderstandings that otherwise may occur.

If you would like to read more of my thinking about assessment, all my blog posts on limiting grading can be found at http://pernillesripp. com/major-topics/no-homework-no-grades-no-punishment-resources/ limited-grades/.

I tell my students to speak boldly, and they do. Thank you, Corinne, for letting me share your poem.

Treated As One
1.5, 2.9, 3.4, 4.0
Grade point averages
They define who we are.
People walk around school saying
"I got an A"—4.0
"I have a learning disability"—1.5
"I don't understand"—2.9
"I'm not good enough"—3.4
People always say "Everyone is different"
Well if everyone is different why do we ALL
have to take the same test?
Why do we have one grading system
for six schools with hundreds of kids.
I know life isn't always fair but school should be.
Because school is where you practice
It's where you practice what you'll later need.
Why is a group of different people
taught in one way?
A way where half of the kids don't understand,
and then the teachers have to say to their parents
"They don't put in enough effort"
When maybe they think in a different way
I speak for my dyslexic sister
who has to get tutored two times a week
She has told me many times
"I don't understand"
It's such a sad thing to see a brilliant mind get
shut away because of what the other kids will say
She once had a teacher that said
she used the word dyslexic as an excuse
to get out of reading
When she hadn't even read the papers that diagnose her.
My sister is one out of thousands
who don't get treated fair,
We all just have to live with being
treated as one
All though we are more.

When Change Happens to Good Teachers

"I wish all teachers knew that not all students are alike and most will never be." —Carolyn G.

This Is My Most Precious Moment

He places a picture of his mother who has passed away under the document camera and takes my breath away.

Tears and stammered out questions about the picture. He asks if he may sit down—and the tears keep coming from me, from him, from everyone.

We cannot measure student trust on a test.

We cannot measure the value of a classroom community that allows a kid to share his most precious moment and the emotions that accompany it.

We cannot measure the bravery in that child who was willing to be so vulnerable.

We cannot measure the connection the other kids felt when they saw how much this meant to him.

None of that gets measured on a test.

None of that will ever be a part of my educator effectiveness evaluation.

Not the tears. Not the unique moments. Not the trusting and caring we feel for each other.

No one knows how to measure it. And so they don't.

And yet, these moments are the ones that make my classroom a community.

They are the reason my students thrive, and grow, and love school. They are the very moments that should count the most.

Instead the assessors focus on math facts, isolated reading skills, the bubbles well-filled.

They pretend these bits of information give them a full picture of this boy.

They pretend that they know the strengths and weaknesses of this kid.

They pretend that this "data" can reveal whether I am good teacher.

We know it doesn't. We know it's a pitiful measure of the boy and of me.

When will the outside world learn? Why don't they pay attention to what matters?

Then: I Did What They Expected Me to Do

"I wish teachers knew how the schools have changed. It's different than when they were in school, like when we go home we aren't that lazy as teachers would think."

—Cylie S.

Five years ago, I realized that I needed to take responsibility for the damage I had done to students who came into my room loving (or at least liking) school and left diminished in some ways. Those kids who loved math until my long-winded lectures about process left them confused and bitter. Those kids who loved to read until my strict book report guidelines and reading logs devoured their curiosity for great stories.

I had to take responsibility for what I had done. There was no one else to blame. Just as important, I had to make sure that my future students would leave our classroom still loving school, with passionate curiosity, not afraid to try something new.

How do we make children hate school so much? I now teach seventh grade, but when I taught fourth I had students who already hated school. By then certain subjects had already landed on their top 10 list of most dreadful things to do. Math tended to top the chart, but social studies was usually close behind, and some even hated reading (but may read many books outside of school). By seventh it seems ~~it seems~~ that the most hated class is writing. Most students confess a love of recess, art, music, and sometimes even science. PE is always a crowd favorite as well, unless homework or writing is involved. Yet, students typically do not come to school hating certain classes; it is what we do to them in those classes that make them hate school.

I don't blame the students. The system of school has taught them to feel this way. How dare I say this? Because I was that system. I think about math and how I taught it: drill and kill, lecture and lecture some more. Show them repeatedly how to do a problem, then have one or two students come up and work through a similar problem while the rest of the class watches (eyes glazing over). And finally have them practice it on their own, usually through homework. In my straight-edged classroom, students were not allowed to work ahead—they needed to pay attention to me, slogging through all of the pages. We did not have much time for discussion, let alone any further exploration.

Substitute *social studies* for *math* in the paragraph above, leave out the problems at the board, and you have a pretty good summary of what my social studies class looked like as well. By the time I was done teaching, my students were good at putting their names on worksheets, filling them out, and following along in the textbook. Too bad about their curiosity. We just didn't have time for that.

So I changed. And if you want to change but haven't tried yet, take my word for it—you can too. I'm not that special; lots of teachers are changing the way they teach and how school is done. Many did not wait for permission but transformed on their own. If you would like someone's permission, you hereby have mine. Go ahead—start to create your own classroom of passionate learners.

I will admit that not every kid leaves my classroom having fallen back in love with school. Sometimes that damage takes years to undo. But I get them started on the path of loving learning again. I take responsibility for my own actions as a teacher and realize

> If you want to change but haven't tried yet, take my word for it—you can too.

the damage I can do. I go to school knowing that every day I can be the difference between a child embracing his or her own learning or tuning out. I accept that what I do today may make the difference a few years from now between staying in school or dropping out.

Now: I Do What My Students Need Me to Do. And So Can You

"Being a student is hard. You don't have much time to do the stuff you love."
—Addison Z.

I believed that there was one way to do school to kids. Now I know that school needs to change, and we have to change it from within. Part of that change needs to be about including the voices of our students. School can no longer just be done to our kids; kids must experience it and own it.

> School can no longer just be done to our kids; kids must experience it and own it.

When I first started on this journey of changing the way I teach, I did not know where my path would ultimately lead. I still don't. With every child who enters my classroom, and with every parent who comes along with something to share, that path changes and so must I.

I set out to give the classroom back to the students, and this remains my mission, yet I have not accomplished all of the goals I set for myself. With any change there comes resistance, and I have met my fair share. Students who did not understand why they couldn't just be told how to do something. Parents who felt I didn't give enough homework or enough grades. Teachers who thought I wasn't doing a good enough job preparing the kids. My own doubt sneaking in whenever an idea did not work.

Yet, if we want to make change, we must expect to fight for what we believe in—even with ourselves sometimes. There are ways that we can change our school system from within, even though many policy makers may seem to work against us.

I asked my students what they wanted from school, and the one thing that came up time and time again was choice. For them to have voice in how they learn. For learning to become fun again. So here are 10 simple ways that you can give students a voice, starting tomorrow.

1. Give Them a Blog

My students have blogged since 2010 and nowhere do I see the global effects of them having a voice in a bigger way. Our blogs serve not just as a way to record our growth but as a way to start a dialogue with the world. And my students embrace it because we take the time to do so. They see the results in their comments. They see how people react. Blogging has changed the way I teach more than once.

2. Give Them Time

Student voice takes time, at least the type of voice that will lead to changes. So invest the time in the beginning, model what your conversations will look like, and take the time to showcase the tools they will use. Student voice is something I come back to throughout the year because students often forget that we want to hear their opinions, simply because they are not used to someone asking (and listening). So make it a focus and keep it in focus all year.

3. Give Them Sticky Notes

Wondering how you will engage your shy students? Wondering how you are going to find time for this? Have them write down their idea on a sticky note and hand it to you. Often some of my strongest students are the ones who have the hardest time speaking up, and yet student voice does not necessarily mean the words have to be spoken. They have to be communicated, and sticky notes count as that. In fact, this is something that I use throughout the year as a quick way to check opinion. Students can express their honesty without wondering about judgment from others.

4. Model Constructive Feedback

Part of student voice is getting and giving constructive feedback. If students want to change the way things are done well, then they need to know how to approach it. Often students can be overly blunt, which requires a thick skin, but take the time to discuss how to frame their words so they will be listened to. I teach my students that how they deliver their message sometimes matter more than the actual message; you can get so much further with kindness.

5. Give Them Whiteboards

One of the easiest ways I have for including all student voices within the class (beside sticky notes) are two-dollar whiteboards, massive white shower walls cut into smaller sizes and accessible at any time. Sometimes students flash their answers to me while others are still working it through, sometimes they use them to brainstorm and walk around showing each other, other times they write on them and then leave them for me to read after class is over. Why not just use paper? There seems to be something about paper that often inhabits kids, the whiteboard though with its quick-erase capabilities allow kids to express even half-complete thoughts and take more risks.

6. Give Them a Chance

Student voice is not something that develops as a class culture by itself. It has to be a focused approach to include all voices and there is bound to be not-so-stellar moments. Yes, your feelings will probably get hurt (mine still do), Yes, students will say cringe-worthy things. Yes, students may even hurt each other's feelings or be misunderstood. But if you persist in it, working through any obstacles, you will see the results.

7. Give Them an Audience

While student voice kept within a classroom can be quite powerful in itself, find a way for students to connect with the world so that their voice can be amplified. Blog, tweet, Skype, use whatever tools you have available even if they don't include tech, but give students the opportunity to make a difference to a larger crowd than their classroom. The give-and-take process that happens between an audience and the students is something that will teach them even bigger lessons about delivering a message and getting their point across.

8. Give Them a Starting Point

Sometimes my students are eager to share all of their opinions and ideas, and other times they are not. So provide all students with a common starting point. I always start by asking questions specific to what we are doing and how they would like to change it. (Don't forget to listen to it and change the things you can!) Then move forward from there, making the issues deeper until students are sharing comfortably. A few months in I know I can start to ask my students more personal questions and have them share their answers because they have shown me they are ready.

9. Give Them a Purpose

My students want to change the world. Well, at least some of them do. So I try to get out of their way. Whether I ask them to look for things they can change locally or globally or it grows naturally out of whatever we are doing, once that seed has been planted, it often does not take much for students to get involved. Even within our confined schedules there are many ways to tie our standards into service learning.

10. Give Them Trust

I think we fear that students will say stupid things (they might). I think we fear that students will make fools out of themselves (they won't). I think we have so many fears when it comes to giving students a voice that we often don't even try it because we know all of the things that can go wrong. But what if we started in a place of hope rather than a place of fear? I hope my students will change the world. I hope my students will find their voice matters. I hope my students will have the courage to tell me how to be a better teacher for them. But I won't know unless they try. We are here to protect and guide them, yes, but we are also here to watch them unfold their wings. At some point we have to let go; at some point we have to trust them.

So How Do We Change?

"Take the time to get to know your students and see how they learn best."

—Eleni Y.

The one question from teachers I seem to get the most is this: how do you change?

The answer for me has always been: start where you are. Once you embrace the idea that there has to be something better, you are on your way. Take stock of what makes you tick and what makes you stop. What burns you out, and what do you have power over? There are many things that wear my soul down that I cannot control. So I try to focus on the things I can make decisions about. What is in my control? Homework, grades, punishment, the ways information is presented, the community building, the shared ownership.

Then I focus on the few things that I feel ready to change right now. I never marry an idea; I date it. Year after year my ideas should evolve to match my growing understanding and experience. I won't get stuck. I just need to stay focused on my ultimate purpose: to have students love school. Change may always be a constant in education, and I am at peace with that.

What matters in the end is that we did try to change and we did try to right our wrongs. We don't punish ourselves, but we recognize that once we understand that what we've done in the past was hurtful to children, we cannot do it again.

We fight for change within our system, and we fight for our students by giving them a voice to fight with. Some educators say that they are tired of fighting. No one will ever listen to us. This, they say, is the end of education. Reform has gotten so far out of hand that there is no more room for common sense, for creative thinkers, or for partnerships.

People say our students suffer at the hands of all of this reform, and I agree much of the time. What I don't agree with is the belief that there is simply no way to make a difference. I hear teachers say that there will never be productive change, just more tests, more papers, more being "done to"—more, more, more, and always with less.

I say there is hope. That among all of this fear, all of this uncertainty and poorly considered reform, we can still look at our students and see them rise. They know we suffer through testing with them. We can teach them to be resilient. We teach them that sometimes life asks you to do things that make no sense, and we must get through it with grace, courage, and creativity. We can still teach them to love true learning.

So when it all seems to be too much, too dictated, too little too late, think of the students. Think of their potential to be passionate learners. Think of the good we can do for them every day when they enter our schools,

> Among all of this fear, all of this uncertainty and poorly considered reform, we can still look at our students and see them rise.

when we tell them good morning, when we end the day by saying thank you. Thank you for being part of our room, for being part of something bigger than you, for placing your faith in me as your teacher, and for fighting for change by speaking out.

So have hope. Because our students do, day after day. They hope we will build a community with them and that school will become about them again.

Next: What You Can Do, Starting Today

I am continually awed by the incredible educators I get to teach and learn with every day, in my school and in my networks. I am renewed in my already strong belief that we are the change.

We are the change for all of those children whose lives have been determined by assumptions, circumstance, and test scores outside of their control.

We are the change for all of those teachers who don't think they have a voice. You do. Although you may just be one person, there are so many things you can do to change the system. Bring the focus back on the kids, improve teaching conditions, and keep our students passionate and curious.

Give them a voice within your room so that the whole school may hear them. Connect their voices globally so that the whole world may hear them. My students started blogging five years ago and have now had more than 500,000 visitors to their blog. They have an audience to speak to; they have someone other than me who will listen, and that is important.

Stand up for yourself and your beliefs; *they matter, and so do you*, to quote the inspirational author and consultant Angela Maiers.

Speak up, because as each voice joins the chorus, we become louder.

Blog, write to your paper, talk to your community, start a conversation and spread the word. Change will come if we continue to fight for it.

Join together—enough of this us versus them debate. Enough with tearing other teachers down. Show me a perfect teacher, and I will show you 10 people who disagree. We are not perfect, nor should we ever think we are; embrace each other and stand together; this is not just for us but for the kids.

Try your ideas, steal my ideas, and then be proud if they work. Be proud if they fail for at least you tried something.

Believe in them, believe in you, and believe in your team. Be the change. Be the change. Be the change.

You may be just one, but think of how far one person's words can go, the ripples they can start, the waves they can become.

In 2010 I created the Global Read Aloud, hoping that children around the world would connect their lives through a shared read aloud. Now more than 500,000 students have listened to the same stories and realized that the world is, indeed, a small place. I never set out to create a global project, but it happened because I had the courage to try something big, after taking the big step to change myself.

So take your idea and your need for change and do something with it. It is not too late to reinvent yourself, not too late to make a difference. And if you are *just* starting out, don't start the way I did.

Start out right.

Be the change.

Give the classroom back to your students.

Appendix

Student Questionnaire—Beginning of Year

Name _____

Tell Me a Little Bit About Yourself

1. What are the three most important things I should know about you?
    _____
    _____
    _____
    _____

2. What are things you are really good at?
    _____
    _____
    _____
    _____

3. What is the favorite thing you did this summer?
    _____
    _____
    _____
    _____

4. What have you most loved learning (even if not in school)? Why?
    _____
    _____
    _____
    _____

5. What's your favorite thing to do when you're not in school?
    _____
    _____
    _____
    _____

6. What is the best book or books you have ever read?

_____

_____

_____

_____

7. What do you want to learn HOW to do?

_____

_____

_____

_____

8. I think seventh grade will be . . .

_____

_____

_____

_____

9. What do you love about school?

_____

_____

_____

_____

10. What do you not like about school?

_____

_____

_____

_____

11. I work best in a classroom or with a teacher that is . . .

_____

_____

_____

_____

12. Some things I really want to work on this year in seventh grade are . . .

_____

_____

_____

_____

13. What do you wish teachers would notice about you?

_____

_____

_____

_____

Parent Questionnaire—Beginning of Year

Name _____

Child's Name _____

Tell Me a Little Bit About Your Child

1. What is the most important thing I should know about your child?

_____
_____
_____
_____

2. What is your child passionate about?

_____
_____
_____
_____

3. What would you love your child to get better at?

_____
_____
_____
_____

4. Overall, how does your child feel about school and this grade?

_____
_____
_____
_____

5. My child learns best when the teacher is . . .

_____
_____
_____
_____

6. Great friends for my child are . . .

_____

_____

_____

_____

7. My child does not work well when . . .

_____

_____

_____

_____

8. What is your child's favorite book?

_____

_____

_____

_____

9. Which fears does your child have? (Big or small)

_____

_____

_____

_____

10. What is the best way to motivate your child?

_____

_____

_____

_____

Tell Me a Little Bit About You and Your Family

1. What are you looking forward to with this grade?

_____

_____

_____

_____

2. How would you like to be involved with your child's education?

_____

_____

_____

_____

3. What is your preferred method of communication (email, phone call, meeting, note . . .)

_____

_____

_____

_____

4. Does your family have any special celebrations or traditions you would like to share with the class?

_____

_____

_____

_____

5. What subject/area did you dislike when you went to school?

_____

_____

_____

_____

6. What subject/area did you love when you went to school?

_____

_____

_____

_____

7. I think this year will be . . .

_____

_____

_____

_____

8. A typical afternoon after school looks like this in our life . . .

_____

_____

_____

_____

9. Who else lives at your house (siblings, pets etc.)?

_____

_____

_____

_____

10. Anything else you would like to tell me that will help me make this a successful year?

_____

_____

_____

_____

50-Day Class Reflection

Name—if you want to put it on here : _____

What are your thoughts on this class this year—do you like it?
Do you like the way I teach? Why or why not?
What do you really dislike in this class?
What do you really like about this class?
What do you wish I wouldn't do?
Do you feel respected by the teacher?
Do you feel like your voice matters in this class, like your ideas are heard?
Would you consider yourself a good student in this class? Why or why not?

Do you use your time well in this class? Why or why not?
What do you wish would change in this class?
How do you wish I would change?
Overall, do you like being a student in this class?
Anything else?

Quarter 1 Self-Reflection and Grades

Name _____   Hour _____

Proficiency level	Descriptor	Explanation
4	Exceeds expectations or Exemplary	The student demonstrates a deeper level of understanding and a deeper application of skills or analysis of the content beyond grade level expectations.
3	Fully Proficient, meets expectations	Student has fully demonstrated content mastery and skill application of the outcomes for the particular summative assessment at this point in the school year. **This is the expected level of performance.**
2	Partial mastery/ still progressing	The student has demonstrated partial mastery of the expected content/skills in the assessment. Partial development indicates a progress with gaps in understanding or perhaps misconceptions. Progress means not yet fully meeting the expected grade level performance.
1	Minimal understanding/ effort shown	Little or no evidence of content mastery of outcomes. Student has large gaps in understanding/ application and is able to show success only with significant adult assistance.

| IE | Insufficient Evidence | The assessment was not completed or turned in, or there was not enough evidence available for the teacher to determine a score. |

Standard covered	When did we cover this?	Your grade—and why

How many books have you read for the 25-book challenge?	
What did you accomplish this quarter?	
What do you really need to work on?	
What are you really proud of this quarter?	
What is your first goal for 2nd Quarter and how will you reach it?	
What is your second goal for 2nd Quarter and how will you reach it?	
What is your third goal for 2nd Quarter and how will you reach it?	
Anything else you want to share with me?	

Student Questionnaire—End of Year

Name _____

1. Was this grade a good year for you?
   _____
   _____
   _____
   _____

2. Did you feel I was fair? Why or why not?
   _____
   _____
   _____
   _____

3. Did you feel respected by me? Why or why not?
   _____
   _____
   _____
   _____

4. Was I a good teacher for you? Why or why not?
   _____
   _____
   _____
   _____

5. Did you have enough homework or practice?
   _____
   _____
   _____
   _____

6. Did you get enough help?
   _____
   _____
   _____
   _____

7. How prepared do you feel for the next year?

_____
_____
_____
_____

8. Did you feel safe in the classroom?

_____
_____
_____
_____

9. Which projects/learning did you love?

_____
_____
_____
_____

10. Which projects/learning did you dislike?

_____
_____
_____
_____

11. What should I change in my classroom set up?

_____
_____
_____
_____

12. What should I change in how I teach?

_____
_____
_____
_____

13. What should I never teach again?

_____

_____

_____

_____

14. What should I spend more time on?

_____

_____

_____

_____

15. What is the one thing you are always going to remember from this grade?

_____

_____

_____

_____

16. What rule or routine did you not like for most of the year?

_____

_____

_____

_____

17. What are two specific things I need to change?

_____

_____

_____

_____

18. If you could give advice to my new students, what would you say?

_____

_____

_____

_____

Parent Questionnaire—End of Year

Name _____

1. What are your thoughts on the weekly newsletter?
   _____
   _____
   _____
   _____

2. Did you receive adequate communication this year?
   _____
   _____
   _____
   _____

3. Was our class blog helpful to you?
   _____
   _____
   _____
   _____

4. How could I have better supported your child in his or her social development?
   _____
   _____
   _____
   _____

5. How do you feel that your child responded to not receiving extrinsic rewards in class?
   _____
   _____
   _____
   _____

6. How could I have better supported your child in his or her academic development?

_____
_____
_____
_____

7. How could I have better communicated your child's academic goals and challenges?

_____
_____
_____
_____

8. Was I accessible to you when the need arose?

_____
_____
_____
_____

9. How did you feel about the level of homework?

_____
_____
_____
_____

10. How could I have better prepared your child for the next grade?

_____
_____
_____
_____

11. Is there anything that you thought was particularly effective or enjoyable for child?

_____
_____
_____
_____

12. Is there anything that I could work on doing differently next year?

_____

_____

_____

_____

13. How could I improve my teaching next year?

_____

_____

_____

_____

Fall Conference Sheet for Elementary School Teachers

Student Name: _____ Adult name(s):_____

Time:

B = Beginning   D = Developing   S = Secure

Individual Development	B	D	S	Comments
Exhibits self-control/is respectful to others				
Organizes materials/space				
Follows directions (oral or written)				
Completes work accurately (to the best of one's ability)				
Completes work on time				
Listens attentively				
Works independently/Uses time wisely				
Participates in class discussion				
Reads with focus/stamina				
Social behaviors and cooperative group work				
Self-advocates				

Subject	Strength	Goals
Reading		
Writing		
Math		
Science		
Social Studies		

Goals for the rest of the year:

Fall Conference Sheet for Middle School Teachers

Name _____ Hour _____

Strengths:

Goals:

Standards Covered	Grade
1: Determine and analyze the development of central ideas/themes in a text; summarize.	
3: Analyze how story elements interact.	
7: Draw evidence from texts to support written analysis.	
8: Command the conventions of standard English grammar, usage, and vocabulary.	

Name _____ Hour _____

Strengths:

Goals:

Standards Covered	Grade
1: Determine and analyze the development of central ideas/themes in a text; summarize.	
3: Analyze how story elements interact.	
7: Draw evidence from texts to support written analysis.	
8: Command the conventions of standard English grammar, usage, and vocabulary.	

Spring Conference Sheet for Teachers

Child:
    Parents:
    Time:

    Academic strengths:

    Personal strengths:

    Academic goals:

    Personal goals:

    Next year specific goals:

My Conference Sheet for Student Prep

Name:
    Date and time conference is:

    Reading

    My favorite book so far and why:

    How much reading do I do?

    What are my goals as a reader?

    What have I accomplished so far as a reader?

What would I like to accomplish as a reader in fifth grade (long-term goal?)

How is what we are doing in reading helping me become a better reader in life?

Writing

What are your current writing goal(s):

I do this really well in writing . . .

I am still working on this in writing . . .

Is writing easy or hard for you? _____ Why?

I would really like to accomplish this in writing . . .

Math

A concept that I have really understood is:

This is really easy for me in math . . .

This is something I really work on in math:

Work Habits and Behavior

So far in this grade I have grown in these areas:

When I am given a challenge, I . . .

My attitude so far in this grade has been _____ because:

How do you feel about your friendships?

When there is homework due, I make sure to . . .

When something doesn't go the way I want it to, I . . .

When I need help, I . . .

When we discuss as a class or group, I . . .

I wish my teachers would help me with . . .

I wish my parents/guardians would help me with . . .

I wish my teachers would notice . . .

I wish my parents would notice . . .

I wish my friends would notice . . .

Fifth grade would be easier if I . . .

Please write three goals for the rest of fifth grade:

1.

2.

3.

Other information I want to share:

Student Preparation Sheet for Conferences

This is to help you prepare for your student-led conference; however, any of it can be used at your conference.

Name:
Date and time conference is:

Reading:
Have a current book ready to share and discuss.

My reading goal(s): _____
_____
_____

How much reading do I do?
_____
_____
_____
_____

Which reading strategies have I worked on?
_____
_____
_____
_____

What do I do as a great reader?
_____
_____
_____
_____

Writing:

Have two samples of your recent writing ready to share.

What is your writing goal(s):

_____

_____

_____

_____

How are you a great writer?

_____

_____

_____

_____

What are you working on in writing?

_____

_____

_____

_____

Math:

Math facts:

Start of trimester Now

+

−

×

/

What has been your favorite unit and why?

_____

_____

_____

_____

What are your strengths in math?

_____

_____

_____

_____

What are your goals for math?

_____

_____

_____

_____

Science:

What are we currently learning about?

_____

_____

_____

_____

What has been your favorite unit and why?

_____

_____

_____

_____

Be prepared to do a mini-demonstration of (add what the child will be demonstrating if anything) . . .

Social Studies:

What are we currently studying?

_____

_____

_____

_____

Where in history are we and why are we learning about it?

_____

_____

_____

_____

What has been your favorite unit and why?

_____

_____

_____

_____

Personal skills:

I am a _____

I need to work on _____

I hand in my homework _____

Please write three goals for the rest of the year:

1. _____

_____

2. _____

_____

3. _____

_____

Spring Student Conference Reflection

Name:

Time and date of conference:

As we get ready for next year, we need to reflect on ourselves as learners. Please write down as much as you can about yourself as a learner and as a person. Questions to consider in each subject area are:

◆ What are your goals for the rest of this grade?
◆ What are your goals in general?
◆ How have you grown already?
◆ What do you need to still work on?
◆ What are some of your accomplishments?
◆ Anything else you want to share.

Reading Reflection:

Writing Reflection:

Math Reflection:

Science Reflection:

Social Studies Reflection:

Me as a learner:
What have you accomplished in this grade, what have you failed at but grown from, what are things you have to fix before middle school, how are you ready for middle school, and anything else you can add:

How can my parents help me in school?

How can I get ready for next year?

Parent Post-Conference Questionnaire

Please complete this after your child's student-led conference and hand in to (insert name) by (insert day).

Name:

	Strongly agree	*Agree*	*Disagree*	*Strongly disagree*
I left the conference with a deeper understanding of my child's academic growth.				
My child was well prepared and was able to communicate their goals clearly.				
I enjoyed the format of the conference.				
The teacher provided me with the information needed to understand my child's strengths and goals.				
I feel there is a plan in place to ensure the continued academic growth of my child.				

Additional comments:

Common Misbehaviors and How We Work With Them

Misbehavior	Old Ways	New Ideas for Teachers
A child constantly blurts or interrupts	Reprimand, check mark or anything else that signals they were not following rules	◆ Partner share—have them tell answers to children at their tables before sharing with you ◆ Dry erase board—this way they can flash you the answer rather than blurt it out ◆ A tally sheet—They mark down when they blurt out to create awareness of problem. At the end of the lesson students have a visual for how much they blurt out and a conversation can be had discussing the amount.
The child who cannot sit still	Force them to "Pay attention!"	◆ Give them a movement break—a quick walk around the school usually helps. I also have students stand and pace in the back if that helps them absorb the learning better. ◆ Allow them to work wherever they choose, at least then they will not distract their seat mates ◆ Change up the way you are teaching ◆ Access to different types of seating such as ball chairs, stand-up desks, or anything else you can get your hands on ◆ A basket of fidgets for anyone who needs to borrow one—they can grab one when they walk in, leave it when class is over

(*Continued*)

Situation	Reaction	Strategies
The class that cannot concentrate	Yell or raise voice, give them a lecture about importance of information	◆ Change the way something will be taught ◆ Ask the students how they would like to learn about it ◆ Give them a brain break and ask them to re-focus once break is over
Late or missing homework	Missed recess or phone call home, loss of privileges	◆ Ask them how they plan to fix it. Often students will brainstorm a way to get it done. ◆ If they say they left it at home tell them you believe them and that they can hand it in the following day ◆ Conference to set up plan for remembering in the long run ◆ Digging a little deeper: why is homework not being done? Is it due to organization, need for more information/inability to complete, or outside influences?
Disrespect	Yelling or raised finger, immediate dismissal to office	◆ Much of this can be prevented through establishment of community, however, if it happens, stay calm, try to alleviate the situation by using humor privately with the student, and take a breath before reacting. ◆ Speak privately to the student about the disrespect and ask for reasons behind it ◆ Spend a moment every day asking that student two questions about their life, stick with it to see a better relationship form

Constant chatting between students or passing notes	Singling out students, loss of privilege	◆ Offer students two minutes at some point during the class to let them just speak about whatever they want.
		◆ Recognizing the conversation and asking them to stop then changing how the lesson is delivered if it is excessive.
		◆ Give students time to discuss or work with partners
		◆ Ignore behavior if it is not a big deal—does time need to be spent on it?
Excessive violation of classroom rules	Loss of privileges, loss of recess, sent to the office	◆ Classroom discussion to see if rules need to be changed to better fit the needs of all students; small tweaks or individual changes can go a long way.
		◆ Ask children why they are doing what they are doing and what you can do to help.
		◆ Keep it low key to not give it more importance and trying to figure out what is causing it rather than just focusing on the infractions themselves.

Would I Like Being a Student in My Own Classroom? A Teacher Tool for Reflection

Community

Answer yes or no to these questions.

Do I greet every student with a smile?	
Do I use the name of each child at least once during a day or a lesson?	
Do I ask my students about their personal lives?	
Do I notice when students are out of sorts?	
If a child seems out of sorts, do I find the time to reach out to him or her?	
Do any of my old students ever contact me, either in-person or through tools such as email, blogging, Facebook, or letters?	
Do I laugh with my students?	
Am I always in a hurry?	
Can students state their opinions/ give feedback without me retaliating?	
Do my students trust me?	

What stands out?

_____

_____

_____

_____

Things I am proud of:

_____

_____

_____

_____

Things I may want to change:

_____

_____

_____

_____

Environment

Answer yes or no to these questions.

Are there different areas for students to work in?	
Do students have a choice where they work?	
Do students have a choice in how they work?	
Is my classroom inviting to all genders?	
Am I represented in the room?	
Are my students represented in the room?	
Is the room useful?	
Can students access tools they need without asking such as pencils, staples, etc.?	
Can students move furniture as needed?	
Do the students take ownership over the room?	

What stands out?

_____

_____

_____

_____

Things I am proud of:

_____

_____

_____

_____

Things I may want to change:

_____

_____

_____

_____

Lesson Planning and Doing

Answer yes or no to these questions.

Do I understand the end goal of my lessons?	
Do the students understand the end goal of lessons?	
Do my lessons build off each other?	
Do we have a path planned that leaves rooms for student input?	
Do my students have any choice in what they are doing?	
Is there a way to assess what they learn through conversation?	
Do my lessons always require a grade?	
Are students ever given a chance to re-do something?	

Do students ever decide their own grade or assessment?	
Do I ask for feedback from students either before, during or after a unit is complete?	

What stands out?

_____
_____
_____
_____

Things I am proud of:

_____
_____
_____
_____

Things I may want to change:

_____
_____
_____
_____